What Life Was Like®

AMONG DRUIDS AND HIGH KINGS

Celtic Ireland
AD 400 ~ 1200

What Life Was Like

AMONG DRUIDS AND HIGH KINGS

Celtic Ireland
AD 400 ~ 1200

BY THE EDITORS OF TIME-LIFE BOOKS, ALEXANDRIA, VIRGINIA

CONTENTS

among druids and high kings

Ireland's Celtic Heritage

Five hundred years before the birth of Christ, the Celtic peoples of Europe first appear in the historical record. Referred to as *Keltoi* by the ancient Greeks, they were tribes of warrior-farmers who spread from their homelands in central Europe to Italy, Greece, the Balkans, and Asia Minor, as well as France (Gaul), Spain, Britain, and Ireland.

Although the Celts established cultural dominance over much of this vast realm, they never formed a political empire, and during the second century BC they came under increasing pressure from the growing power of Rome. In 52 BC, Gaul—the last Celtic stronghold on the Continent—fell to the legions of Julius Caesar, and by the end of the first century AD, Rome controlled all of Europe and most of Britain.

Only Ireland escaped Roman occupation. A Roman general stationed in western Scotland is said to have declared that a mere legion backed by a small force of auxiliaries would be sufficient to conquer the island. But Ireland was never invaded by the Romans and thus endured as a surviving bastion of Celtic civilization.

Relatively undisturbed by outside influences, the Celtic way of life flourished in Ireland until the arrival of Christianity in the fifth century. Knowledge of the pagan Celts is incomplete, and they remain, as one historian puts it, "like figures perceived through a mist and heard very faintly." What *is* known about them is derived mainly from Irish sagas and tales, which were passed down by oral tradition until they

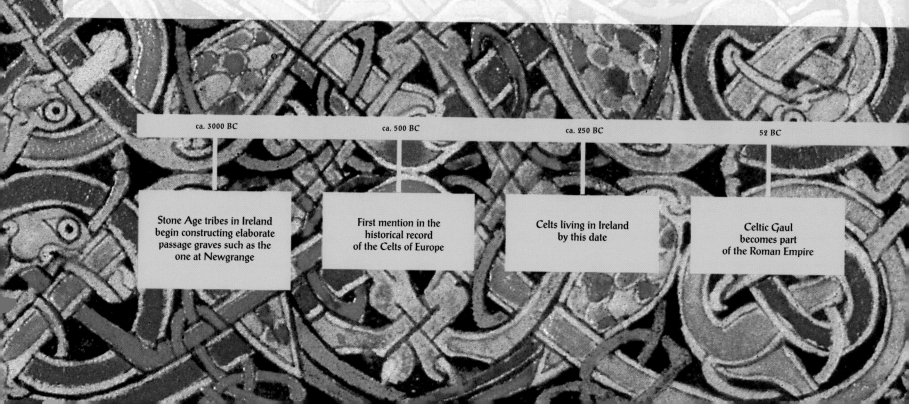

ca. 3000 BC

Stone Age tribes in Ireland begin constructing elaborate passage graves such as the one at Newgrange

ca. 500 BC

First mention in the historical record of the Celts of Europe

ca. 250 BC

Celts living in Ireland by this date

52 BC

Celtic Gaul becomes part of the Roman Empire

were recorded during the seventh and eighth centuries. The sagas speak of warrior-kings such as Tara's Cormac Mac Airt and Ulster's Connor Mac Nessa, of wicked queens like Maeve of Connacht, and of great champions like Cu Chulainn. The tales also describe an exotic world of beautiful women and magical beasts; of the druids and poets who guarded Irish lore, law, and religion; and of sorcery and enchantment and the gods of pagan Ireland.

During this so-called heroic age, Irish chieftains began to prey on Roman Britain, launching well-organized raiding parties that swooped down on the British coast and carried off booty and slaves. One such raid brought back to Ireland a teenager who would eventually change the country forever:

Patricius Magonus Sucatus, or as he would be known later, Saint Patrick.

The Ireland to which Patrick came was populated by fewer than half a million inhabitants, each bound by a basic system of customary law and social hierarchy. The Irish appear to have been particularly receptive to the gospel message, which traveled quickly across the land. And as it did so, the old religion of the druids died out, although its traces would linger in ancient festivals turned into holy days and pagan gods transformed into Christian saints.

The island at this time was wholly rural, lacking the towns or cities that had developed in other parts of Europe. Thus, as Christianity spread in Ireland in the century after Patrick, it

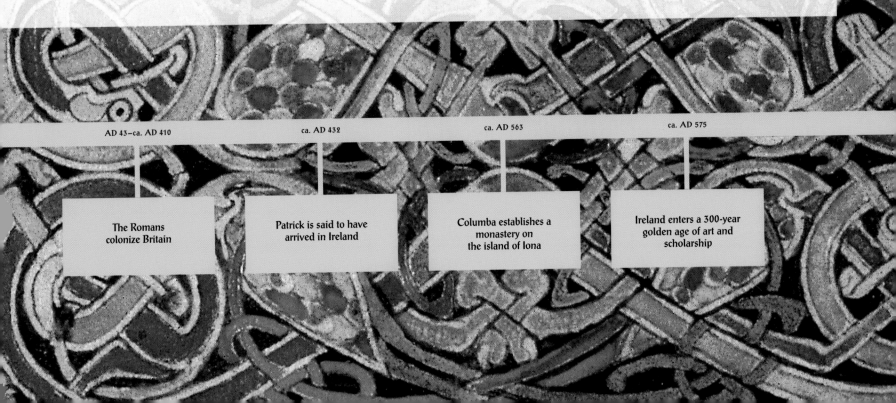

AD 43–ca. AD 410

The Romans colonize Britain

ca. AD 432

Patrick is said to have arrived in Ireland

ca. AD 563

Columba establishes a monastery on the island of Iona

ca. AD 575

Ireland enters a 300-year golden age of art and scholarship

took on a distinctly Irish nature; in the absence of towns, monasteries quickly became important semiurban centers and abbots effective leaders of the church.

These monastic strongholds would provide a beacon of faith for the rest of Europe in the years ahead. Indeed, in the second half of the sixth century Irish monks undertook pilgrimages to the Continent, where they brought the gospel to many still-pagan peoples, founding monasteries at such places as Luxeuil in France, Fosse in Belgium, and Bobbio in Italy. Meanwhile, at home, Ireland entered something of a golden age during which scholarship, art, and literature flowered, and students from abroad flocked to Irish monasteries.

The monasteries also drew other, less welcome foreigners, and in the year 795 Viking longships appeared off the Irish coast. Over the next two centuries, Viking hit-and-run raids on Ireland's monasteries gradually evolved into an organized campaign of conquest and settlement. In 841 the Vikings founded Dublin, their first permanent settlement in Ireland, and later established Cork, Limerick, Waterford, and Wexford. And as they settled, the newcomers intermarried with the Irish and adopted Irish ways. The Vikings (or more accurately, the Irish-Norse) were key players at Clontarf, the great battle fought in 1014 between the Irish high king, Brian Boru, and the kings of Dublin and Leinster. Although the battle is often portrayed as a victory of the Irish over the Norse, both sides were made up of Irish and Viking warriors.

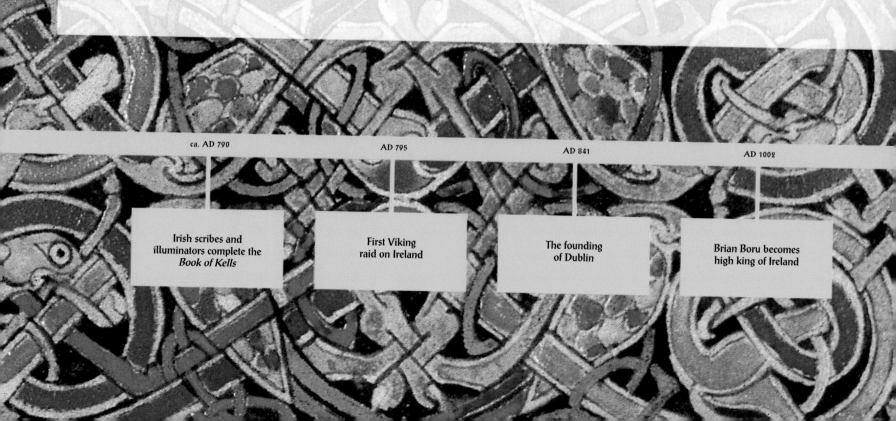

ca. AD 790	AD 795	AD 841	AD 1002
Irish scribes and illuminators complete the *Book of Kells*	First Viking raid on Ireland	The founding of Dublin	Brian Boru becomes high king of Ireland

By Brian Boru's day, the high kingship of Ireland was a prize open to all, and at various times between 1014 and 1169 the kings of Munster, Ulster, Connacht, and Leinster held the position. It was the struggle for the high kingship that ushered in another wave of invasion and conquest, ending forever the prospect of an Irish king ruling over all of Ireland. To bolster his ambitions of becoming high king, Dermot Mac Murrough, king of Leinster, sought foreign help, and in 1168 there arrived in Ireland a force of Anglo-Norman knights, descendants of the Normans who had conquered England a century before. Others were soon to follow. Citing papal backing, Henry II, the Norman king of England, sailed to Ireland in 1171 and claimed the island as his own.

The isolation that had once preserved Celtic Ireland was over, and the age of English colonialism had begun. The Anglo-Normans introduced their own laws and customs and brought the Irish church more into line with the orthodoxy of Rome. But the Normans, like the Vikings and the Christian missionaries before them, were themselves changed even as they set about changing the Irish. The people of Ireland had seen it all before. As their country entered another twilight realm of turmoil and transition, the Irish consoled themselves with their past—with the exploits of their mythological heroes, with the accomplishments of Patrick, Columba, and the saints of the Celtic church, and with tales of what life was like in the time of druids and high kings.

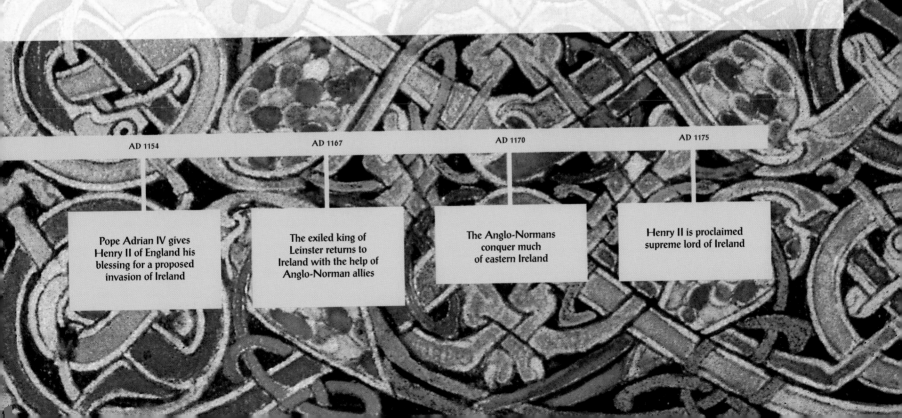

AD 1154

AD 1167

AD 1170

AD 1175

Pope Adrian IV gives Henry II of England his blessing for a proposed invasion of Ireland

The exiled king of Leinster returns to Ireland with the help of Anglo-Norman allies

The Anglo-Normans conquer much of eastern Ireland

Henry II is proclaimed supreme lord of Ireland

Derry

Lough Neagh

ULSTER

Armagh
Emain Macha
Downpatrick

CONNACHT

Croagh Patrick

Monasterboice
Kells
Newgrange
MEATH
Uisneach
(Navel of Ireland)
Boyne River
Tara

Durrow
Clonmacnoise
River
Clonfert
Clontarf
Dublin

ARAN ISLANDS

Poulnabrone

Kildare
Liffey River

Glendalough
Wicklow
LEINSTER

Shannon
Limerick

Arklow
Slaney River

Ardagh
Lough Gur

Cashel

MUNSTER

Suir River
Wexford

Waterford

Paps of Anu
Lee River
Cork

SKELLIG MICHAEL

THE ISLE OF SAINTS AND SCHOLARS

Perched on the edge of the Atlantic Ocean, Ireland became a repository of Celtic culture for a continent conquered by Rome. Although the Romans never occupied the island, over the centuries other European invaders and migrants would make their way to Ireland's shores: Christians from Britain, raiders from Scandinavia, and French-speaking Anglo-Normans from England and Wales.

The map above shows Ireland in relation to its neighbors, while the map at left shows the country's five historical provinces, or Fifths: Ulster in the north, Leinster in the east, Connacht in the west, Munster in the south, and squeezed between Ulster and Leinster, the province of Meath. Each of the four largest provinces—said to meet at the Navel of Ireland—was associated with a particular quality: warfare in the north, affluence in the east, learning in the west, and music in the south.

Ireland's Sacred Landscapes

To the Celtic people of Ireland, the realm of the supernatural and the natural world were inseparable. Spirits and deities inhabited trees, rocks, rivers, bogs, and mountains, imbuing the countryside with sacred significance. The earth itself was considered divine, a mother goddess responsible for the fruitfulness of the land and for the nurturing of the animals that lived upon it. Several locally affiliated Irish pagan goddesses were identified with the earth, among them Áine of County Limerick and Clíodna of Cork. One local earth goddess who seemed to have attained a measure of preeminence among other deities was Anu, described not only as the goddess of prosperity, but also as the mother of the Irish gods. Anu's domain was the province of Munster, where twin hills resembling breasts were named The Paps of Anu *(below);* long ago, piles of stones called cairns were placed at the hilltops to represent her nipples.

Ireland's early residents frequently augmented the sacred natural formations with monumental structures known as megaliths, from the Greek for "great stones." Their original purpose is unknown, but these structures continue to awe and inspire, just as they did when the Celts first came upon them. Adapting the monuments for their own ritual purposes, the Celts and, later, medieval authors produced legends about the sites' origins and purposes. In these tales, these holy places became the dwelling and trysting areas of the gods, portals through which gods and humans could enter the spirit world, and revered destinations for festivals, rituals, and pilgrimage.

At dawn on the winter solstice, the sun shines through a special opening above the entrance to Newgrange and penetrates one of its interior chambers *(left)*. One of the most magnificent megalithic structures in Europe, the mound is constructed of stones weighing about 4,000 tons, covered with earth and partly surrounded by huge curbstones and smaller white quartz pebbles.

the otherworld

Among the ancient megalithic structures that dot the Irish countryside are the enormous man-made mounds known as passage graves, such as the one shown here at Newgrange, built centuries before the arrival of the Celts. According to the melding of history and myth that is Irish lore, when the ancestors of the Irish people came to Ireland from Spain, they fought the last generation of gods still living on the land and drove them underground. These gods were called the Túatha Dé Danaan, and their new underground kingdom was known as the otherworld. The otherworld was accessible through lakes and caves and through passage graves like Newgrange, called sídh. The Dagdha, father king of the otherworld, gave the sídh to the chiefs of the Túatha Dé for use as dwellings.

The otherworld was a land of mystery and contradictions. There, the Dagdha and the other divine beings lived much like the humans above them, even suffering violence and death, yet at the same time, the kingdom of the Túatha Dé Danaan was a paradise of peace and plenty, with endless hunting, drinking, and feasting. For humans, though, the otherworld was a dangerous place and those who dared to visit it might not escape with their lives.

circles of stone

Ireland's megalithic monument builders were a prolific lot. Indeed, the country has more than 1,200 such monuments—not only the enormous passage graves like Newgrange, but also standing stones, stone rows, and stone circles. The megaliths are ancient—many were built in roughly the same period as the Egyptian pyramids. While it is unclear how they were used in either pre-Celtic or Celtic times, these smaller monuments probably also played a role in the rituals of the pagan Irish.

One stone circle, for example, Rannach Crom Dubh *(above)*, is named for the Irish harvest god and may have been a site of some importance. The entrance to the arena aligns with the sunset on Samhain, the most complex festival in the Celtic sacred seasonal cycle. Celebrated on November 1, Samhain marked the return of cattle from higher pastures, the end of summer, and the start of winter and the new year. It was also a time of courtship and weddings. Despite its promise of rebirth and renewal, however, Samhain, a precursor of today's Halloween, was a dangerous time. It was then that the barriers between this world and the next were temporarily removed, allowing spirits and mortals to cross back and forth between the two realms.

the help of the gods

The most dramatic of all Ireland's megaliths are its dolmens, or portal tombs *(left).* Probably built as aboveground grave sites, dolmens, consisting of three to seven upright stones bearing a massive capstone, somewhat resemble giant stone tables. Some of the stones used in the dolmens weigh more than 100 tons and would have required enormous skill and strength to lift and place in their gravity-defying positions. It is understandable, then, that the Irish Celts would attribute divine provenance to these structures.

In Irish legend, gods, though able to perform miraculous tasks like the building of these monumental structures, possessed human failings as well. In their dealings with people, the gods were often weak and spiteful, as well as courageous and generous. Yet the gods did come to the aid of mortals—at least in the legend of the lovers Diarmaid and Gráinne, who eloped on the eve of Gráinne's wedding to the elderly hero Finn. For years the couple eluded the furious groom, thanks to the god Óengus, Diarmaid's foster father, who warned them never to stay more than one night in each spot. The dolmens were their hastily erected refuges, and in tribute were called Diarmaid and Gráinne beds.

The war goddess Macha used her brooch to draw the boundary of Emain Macha *(near left)*, also known as Navan Fort. Among the most sacred sites in Celtic Ireland, it may have been associated with fertility rites. In the hallowed region of Lough Gur *(far left)*, the goddess Áine gave birth, according to Irish legend.

CREATORS AND DESTROYERS

Celtic goddesses were closely linked to the land. But while some goddesses had fairly straightforward roles ensuring the fertility of the earth, people, and livestock, others were complex fusions of creative and destructive forces. Macha, for example, was a goddess who promoted the cultivation of crops, represented the concept of rulership, and was also a goddess of war. Her royal stronghold, Emain Macha *(above)*, was built for her by five brothers with whom she clashed over her right to rule. Macha eventually overcame and enslaved them.

The fertility goddess Áine possessed similar contradictory aspects to her character. Her special province was the Lough Gur area in County Limerick, a locale long thought to be enchanted. On an island in the lake—whose name means "pain"—the goddess would sit on a birthing chair and labor to bring forth the harvest. At other times, however, Áine might symbolize the other end of life's continuing cycle; it was said she would shape-shift into an old hag who brought strife to those who refused her modest demands.

CHAPTER ONE

the winds of change

From atop the 500-foot-high Hill of Tara in the province of Meath, Loégaire could see hills in all of Ireland's four other provinces. Each of those provinces was divided up into a patchwork of petty kingdoms ruled by competing kings and dynasties. But, as Loégaire often reminded himself, there was only one king of Tara, whose seat was this hill in the Boyne Valley, a sacred site dating back thousands of years. And that king was Loégaire himself, head of one of the mightiest of Irish dynasties, the Uí Néill, or as they were later known, the O'Neills.

Still, Loégaire was a worried man. For some time now he had heard whisperings of strange happenings along the Irish coast, just 17 miles away. Rumors of a man passing from kingdom to kingdom spreading tales of a false new religion made the great king uneasy. Though his own realm so far had been immune to the outsider's disturbing influence, Loégaire knew that he could take no chances.

The king summoned to his royal compound a man named Lucet Máel. Lucet Máel was one of the druids of Celtic Ireland, a powerful figure in whom the king placed great trust. Loégaire directed him to perform a ritual known as the *imbas forosna*—"the knowledge that enlightens"—to determine whether this stranger posed any threat to

Despite the attention to detail shown in this 19th-century engraving of two druids, we know little about what they really looked like.

Tara and the supremacy of the O'Neills. Lucet Máel bowed before his king and retired to his own quarters. There, he pulled a piece of raw dog flesh from a leather pouch and began to chew it. He then removed the meat from his mouth and placed it upon a flag-stone just inside the door of his dwelling. Holding his palms in front of him, the druid chanted prayers over the dog flesh, asking for divine guidance in his quest to see into the future. That night he slept with his palms pressed against his cheeks while an attendant kept close watch to make sure he was not disturbed during his nocturnal journey to the otherworld.

When he awoke the next morning, Lucet Máel was highly agitated; his vision had revealed that "a foreign way of life" was about to come to them. Tara would be overtaken by a new kingdom, one with "an unheard-of and burdensome teaching, brought from afar over the seas." Its unstoppable energy would "kill the kings who offered resistance, seduce the crowds, destroy all their gods, banish all the works of their craft, and reign for ever."

And in his dream Lucet Máel had also glimpsed the stranger who would bring to an end the way of life he and his fellow Celts had practiced for countless centuries. He ran from his house and sought out King Loégaire. The king, sensing the man's trepidation, bade Lucet Máel not to hold anything back in telling the results of the imbas forosna.

Speaking in prophetic verse, Lucet Máel recited the following lines:

There shall arrive Shaven-head,
with his stick bent in the head . . .
he will chant impiety
from his table in the front of his house;
all his people will answer "Be it thus, be it thus."

Loégaire might have been puzzled by the sense of the druid's words. But to the chroniclers who wrote of these events hundreds of years later, during the seventh, eighth, and ninth centuries, the meaning was clear enough. And though the conversations they relate were invented, the gist of the tale is true enough. Loégaire and Lucet Máel were real persons, as was the shaven-headed stranger who, by "chanting impiety," overthrew the ancient pagan gods and introduced the "foreign way of life" to Celtic Ireland. The stranger was none other than Patrick, the island's patron saint, and his message, Christianity.

Patrick's missionary work among the Irish, which probably took place around the middle of the fifth century, would indeed change everything, just as Lucet Máel had predicted. But much of the Celtic character of Ireland would endure. Christianity itself would undergo subtle changes as the Irish blended elements of their old religion into the new faith. And the Irish system of kingship would last for centuries, until it was overthrown by the forcible arrival of yet another foreign way of life, this one brought by Anglo-Norman invaders.

Those who fared the worst under the new order, however, were the keepers of the old order—druids like Lucet Máel. As guardians of Irish paganism, druids came second only to kings in terms of power and prestige. A combination of priest, prophet, and astrologer, druids were believed to possess mystical

Druids carried wands, perhaps similar to this one from continental Europe, as symbols of their office.

abilities, which were highly prized by kings, as well as spells, which were greatly feared by enemies. This alone was enough to damn them in the church's eyes. But druids also served as important educators, judges, healers, and keepers of the calendar. Through their vast store of knowledge they were, in the days before Patrick, indispensable to Irish society.

In those pre-Christian times, the culture of Ireland, like that of Celtic Europe, was based largely on oral traditions kept alive by the druids and others. The early Celtic peoples left few records of their thoughts, ceremonies, and way of life until after they had encountered other cultures that put a greater emphasis on the written word. Much of what is known of them, therefore, comes from the chronicles of outsiders. The overall picture that emerges is of a sophisticated and vibrant society, and a religion steeped in ritual and rooted in a reverence for the natural world.

Druidic services often took place outdoors, either at hallowed ancient sites like Tara—Ireland's seat of "all paganism and idolatry," as it is dubbed in an early biography of Patrick—or, when privacy was called for, in sacred groves and clearings hidden deep in the forests. Druids across Europe seem to have had a deep reverence for trees, especially the oak, hawthorn, and yew. But there is no evidence of Irish druids engaging in the human sacrifice that was said to have been practiced on the Continent.

A Roman writer named Lucan described how Caesar discovered a sacred druidic site in Gaul—modern-day France—that may have resembled the places of worship of Ireland's druids: "A grove there was, untouched by men's hands from ancient times, whose interlacing boughs enclosed a space of darkness and cold shade, and banished sunlight from above." On the boughs of the trees, he continued, "birds feared to perch;

in those coverts wild beasts would not lie down; no wind ever bore down upon that wood, nor thunderbolt hurled from black clouds; the trees, even when they spread their leaves to no breeze, rustled among themselves. Water also fell there in abundance from dark springs. The images of the gods, grim and rude, were uncouth blocks, formed of felled tree-trunks. Legend also told that often the subterranean hollows quaked and bellowed, that yew-trees fell down and rose again, that the glare of conflagration came from trees that were not on fire."

Doubtless, it was at such secluded places that initiates into their order were taught the jealously guarded secrets of the druids' craft, a process said to take fully 20 years. Though he probably never witnessed a ceremony performed by druids, Lucan speaks of their "barbarous rites" and "sinister mode of worship." In fact, the druids' secretive ways only served to magnify the awe—and sometimes fear—that they inspired.

Later chroniclers, some of them writing during medieval times, attributed all kinds of powers to the druids. For example, it was claimed that they could affect the weather, causing snowstorms, fog, and even showers of blood and fire. They could erase a person's memory of any particular event by concocting a "drink of forgetfulness." And they could deliver great victories on the battlefield—by casting spells over entire opposing armies, by erecting a so-called druid's fence that protected their own men, and by creating a magic cloak that rendered a warrior invisible. Druids often delivered these spells, it was believed, while standing on one leg, with an arm outstretched and one eye closed, mimicking the posture of a heron.

Divination was certainly an important function of the druids, much as with Lucet Máel and the imbas forosna. But druids probably also used observation of their surroundings—cloud patterns, the stars, the songs of birds, the shape of a tree root—to foretell the future. And through their secret ceremonies, druids were thought to contact the otherworld and communicate with the gods. Medieval Irish tales characterize this otherworld as a land of enchantment and unending joy, a place where sickness and aging were unknown, food and intoxicating drink abundant, and where birds filled the air with music and the very stones sang.

The inhabitants of the otherworld were the Túatha Dé Danaan—the tribe of the goddess Danu, mother of an important family of gods. According to Irish folklore, the Túatha Dé Danaan were a race of people skilled in the arts of druidism and magic who at some time in the distant past came to Ireland from a northern land. Upon arrival they laid claim to the entire island, whose rulers quite naturally took exception. A battle en-

The Romans claimed that druids used magic eggs, made from the hissings of angry serpents, against evil incantations. This one is made of the mineral called serpentine.

sued in which the Túatha Dé were victorious but their king, Núadha, lost an arm. Since a king was required to be physically perfect, Núadha was forced to relinquish his crown to Bres, a man who apparently had many faults, including the most egregious one for a king: a lack of hospitality. The chiefs of the Túatha Dé Danaan grumbled that "their knives were not greased by him, and however often they visited him their breaths did not smell of ale."

Meanwhile, Núadha had been fitted with a silver arm, and when he demanded the return of his throne, the Túatha Dé Danaan flocked back to him. Bres refused to give

Written in a combination of Roman numerals and letters and the Celtic language of Gaul, this 64-month bronze calendar—which dates from the second or first century BC—helped druids select the most propitious days for religious festivals.

it up, however, and called on a rival tribe, the Fomhoire, for help. A fight to the finish seemed inevitable, and Núadha and the Túatha Dé mustered their army at the royal court of Tara.

During a boisterous feast held on the eve of battle, a stranger appeared at the outer gate of the stronghold offering his services to the Túatha Dé Danaan. The sentry questioned his qualifications, "for no one enters Tara without an art."

"I am a wright," the newcomer declared, referring to his boat-making skills.

"We do not require you," answered the sentry firmly. "We have a wright already."

"I am a smith," the man said. But the sentry replied that they had a smith too. Then the newcomer listed all the other skills he possessed—harpist, champion, poet, warrior, sorcerer—only to be told that the Túatha Dé already had masters of each of those fields.

When the stranger asked if they had one person who boasted all those skills, however, the gatekeeper conceded that they did not and recognized him as a master of all the arts. With that, the man vaulted over Tara's formidable ramparts in a single bound and was heartily welcomed by the warriors at the feast. Núadha was so impressed by this remarkable stranger that he relinquished to him command in the coming battle.

The newcomer's name was Lugh, which means "the Shining One," a deity well known throughout the Celtic world. Upon hearing the Gauls describe Lugh as "possessing, or skilled in many arts together," Caesar equated him with the Roman god Mercury. It is no wonder that Lugh, brilliant, handsome, and athletic, should be so revered. Cities all over Europe—León, Spain; Liegnitz (now Legnica) in Poland; and Lyons, France—were named for this Celtic god.

In the next day's battle against the Fomhoire, Lugh seemed to be everywhere at once, overseeing the preparation of the weapons, shepherding the troops of the Túatha Dé, directing the druids to rain fire upon the enemy—and even casting spells himself, "on one foot and with one eye." The slaughter was great on both sides. But under Lugh's leadership, the Túatha Dé Danaan eventually routed the Fomhoire, whose

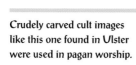

Crudely carved cult images like this one found in Ulster were used in pagan worship.

slain were said to be as many as the stars of heaven, the sands of the sea, the drops of dew upon the grass.

After their victory, Lugh and the Túatha Dé Danaan ruled the island kingdom until they, in turn, met defeat at the hands of the Celts. This time the two warring sides arrived at a compromise, however, and divided the country in two: While the Celts took possession of the upper half, Lugh and the Túatha Dé were relegated to a subterranean realm under the hills of Ireland. There they passed into legend as the residents of the otherworld, living, the Irish believed, "without grief, without sorrow, without death . . . without age, without corruption of the earth."

Scattered throughout the Irish countryside are mounds called sídh. In reality these are ancient burial mounds. But according to Celtic folklore, they were the gateways to the domain of the Túatha Dé. On certain occasions during the year—especially the eve of the feast of Samhain on November 1—spirits from the otherworld were free to leave their sídh to roam the countryside, sometimes with dire consequences for mortals in their path.

Although vestiges of Irish paganism would survive the coming of Christianity, the impact of Patrick and his teaching would change the country profoundly. His mission lasted only about 30 years, but within decades of Patrick's death, Ireland was firmly Christian in character. Many of its kings came to embrace the new religion, and its druids— vilified by Christian clergy and discriminated against by Irish law—faced decline and eventual eclipse.

Despite these accomplishments, the "Shaven-head" of Lucet Máel's prophecy at first remained an obscure figure in his adopted land. No one bothered to save his body after his death, and although the sources strongly suggest that he died in Downpatrick in Ulster, his final resting place remains unknown to this day. Likewise, no one is sure of the date of his birth or his passing. It was only later—posthumously—that his fame grew. In due time the Irish would elevate him to a mythic and legendary status that rivaled that of Lugh himself. But fortunately for us, Patrick left behind an account in his own words that gives some idea of the man and

Three faces appear on this mysterious Irish stone head. Many Celts revered the human head as the soul's dwelling place and ascribed special power to the number three.

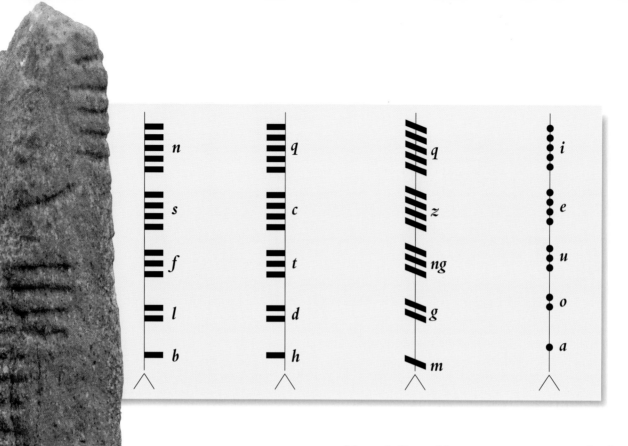

AN IRISH ALPHABET

The edges of this pillar stone are inscribed with characters from an alphabet that was used in fifth-century Ireland. Known as ogham, the 20-letter alphabet was supposedly inspired by Ogma, god of eloquence.

Shown above is a key to ogham; its consonants and vowels can be identified by the number, position, and direction of their notches. The Irish had no other written alphabet until Christian missionaries introduced Latin.

his work. From this we can try to separate the fact from the fiction that surrounds him and catch a glimpse of the real Patrick in the world in which he really lived.

I, Patrick, a sinner, quite uncultivated and the least of all the faithful and utterly despicable to many." These are the first words of Patrick's autobiographical *Confession*, written in his old age when the fruit of his labors must have been evident to him, but also at a time when he faced grave accusations of wrongdoing from elements within his own church.

His words clearly convey one of Patrick's abiding characteristics—humility. The great missionary always felt himself unworthy of any personal laurels for his accomplishments in Ireland, believing he was only doing God's work and making amends for his own misspent adolescence. Yet there is a certain defensiveness in that opening phrase, too, a feeling that his life's labors had been misunderstood by the powers that be. Indeed, perhaps the chance to set the record straight was the driving motivation for a humble man like Patrick to write down his life's story in the first place.

Born in Britain, which at that time was a province of the Roman Empire, he was named Patricius Magonus Sucatus. His grandfather had been a priest (at a time when celibacy was not the rule among the clergy), and his father, a deacon, a member of the town council, and a modestly well-off landowner. But Patrick admits that he himself did not take the teachings of the church to heart. If he had any reverence at all, it was likely for the Roman Empire. Like most Britons, Patrick and his family looked to the legions of Rome for protection from foreign invaders.

Patrick was an indolent youth; in school he paid scant attention to Latin and his other subjects. Then, at the age of 15, as he later confessed in his writings, he committed a grievous sin, one he never felt able to name. Only an extraordinary series of events would turn the young man's life around.

Those events began when Patrick was almost 16 years old. One day, while working at his father's estate, he was seized by raiders and carried off across the sea to Ireland, where he was sold into slavery. For the next half-dozen years, the young man toiled as a shepherd, probably tending his master's flocks on the wind-swept hills near the Atlantic Ocean, or as Patrick knew it, the "Western Sea."

Spending countless days alone in the Irish countryside gave Patrick time to reflect on his life and on the religious lessons he had ignored back home in Britain. "More and more did my love of God and my fear of Him increase," he recalled, "and my faith grew and my spirit was stirred, and as a result I would say up to a hundred prayers in one day, and almost as many at night. I would even stay in the forests and on the mountain and would wake to pray before dawn in all weathers, snow, frost, rain."

Finally one night, after six long years, a voice spoke to him in a dream, telling him it was time to go home. Without hesitation, Patrick slipped away from the flocks and set out on a dan-

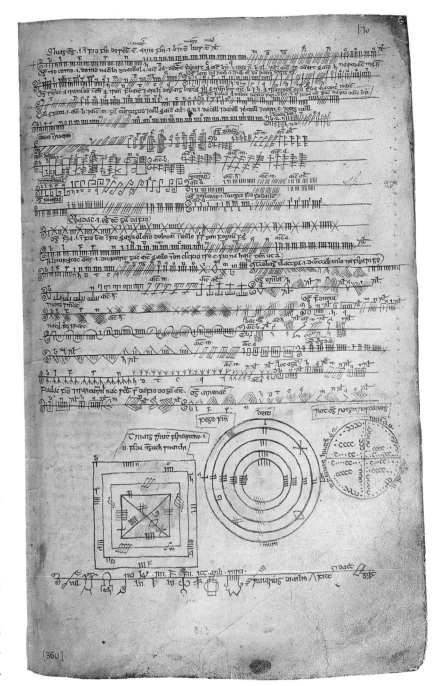

This page comes from the 14th-century *Book of Ballymote*, a manuscript that contains a collection of Irish sagas, law texts, and genealogies, as well as a guide to the ogham alphabet.

gerous 200-mile trek to Ireland's east coast. There he found a cargo ship bound for the European continent. But when he begged for passage aboard the vessel, the captain and crew—"pagans," according to Patrick—brusquely rebuffed his plea for help.

Bitterly dejected, Patrick walked away from the ship and appealed to God for guidance. Before he had even finished his prayer, the crew called him back. "Come, we are taking you on trust," one of them shouted. "Make friends with us in whatever way you wish." The fugitive slave clambered on board, and the ship set sail.

At this point a veil of mystery descends over Patrick's life. His own narrative gives only a fragmentary account of what immediately followed: In three days' time the ship reached land, and Patrick set off with the crew on an overland journey through barren, unpopulated territory. Twenty-eight days later, their food supplies having run out and the men half-dead from hunger, the captain mockingly challenged Patrick. "What about it, Christian?" he taunted. "You say your god is great and all-powerful; well then, why can you not pray for us? We are in danger of starving."

Patrick calmly replied that if the captain would only open his heart to the one true God, all his needs would be provided for. And at that moment,

"a herd of pigs appeared in the way before our eyes." The crew killed them and gorged on the meat for two days until they had recovered their strength. From that moment on, Patrick declared, "I gained great respect in their eyes."

But after describing in detail this month-long ordeal in the wilderness, Patrick's account abruptly jumps forward in time: "And again a few years later I was in Britain with my kinsfolk, and they welcomed me as a son." As to where and how he spent those intervening years he gives no clue. In the 15 centuries since his death, biographers have speculated on his whereabouts and activities during this period, yet no one can say for sure.

Patrick's family gave thanks for his safe return and begged him not to leave them again. But one night he had another dream in which a man handed him a sheaf of letters, and on one of them he read the words "The Voice of the Irish." At that moment, Patrick says, he heard the voices of those in the land of his captivity crying, "We beg you, holy boy, to come and walk again among us."

This vision set Patrick on the course that he would follow for the rest of his life. He determined to study for the priesthood so that he could return to Ireland and preach the gospel to those who had held him in bondage. He studied dili-

A 15th-century carving of Saint Patrick maintains the old legend that he banished snakes from Ireland.

gently, but as he freely admits, he was not—and never would be—a man of letters. And indeed, Patrick's writing provides ample proof that his command of Latin remained rough-hewn throughout his life.

The date of his return to Ireland, like so much else about Patrick, is impossible to pin down. It probably took place around the middle of the fifth century. Already there were small pockets of practicing Christians in the southeast of the island, a result of that region's frequent contact with Britain. When Patrick stepped off the boat, however, the overwhelming majority of the Irish people were still committed to the Celtic gods of their ancestors.

Wisely, Patrick focused his early efforts

Patrick's ministry among the Irish was a remarkable success, and in recognition of this, the church made him bishop of Ireland. With real satisfaction he could declare that "those who never had any knowledge of God but up till now always worshipped idols and abominations are now called the people of the Lord." And with his unfailing modesty, Patrick gave all the credit to God.

But it was in the midst of these successes that Patrick became entangled in a malicious controversy that would overshadow his remaining years. Some, possibly within the church, launched a smear campaign against him, and rumors concerning misappropriation of funds began to make the rounds in British ecclesiastical circles. These accusations seem to have made him genuinely an-

"You say your god is great and all-powerful; well then, why can you not pray for us?"

on converting the local nobility, confident that once the kings embraced Christianity, their subjects would soon follow. And he found that as the kings were won over, they would many times offer a son or daughter to the service of their newfound faith. In this way Patrick was able to train these young nobles and establish an indigenous Irish clergy to spread the word farther.

Patrick also ventured into parts of Ireland where Christians had not dared to go, "where no-one had ever penetrated to baptize or ordain clergy, or confirm the people." During these journeys he faced many dangers, for not all kings were receptive to his message, and the druids, as a class, were understandably hostile. He implies that he was sometimes forced to secure safe passage through certain territories by resorting to bribery. And he declares that he was often saved from martyrdom by a "warning in a divine prophecy."

gry. "When the Lord everywhere ordained clergy through someone as ordinary as me," he wrote, "if I asked any of them for even so much as the price of my shoe, tell it against me, and I shall give it back to you."

His critics even dredged up an incident from Patrick's distant past—the sin he had committed as a 15-year-old. "After 30 years they found a pretext for their allegations against me in a confession which I had made," he recalled. "In a depressed and worried state of mind I mentioned to a close friend what I had done as a boy one day, indeed in the space of one hour, because I was not yet proof against temptation." The friend had revealed Patrick's anguished confession to church investigators, a betrayal that must have saddened him deeply.

Regrettably, it is at this point that the historical record stops. There are no surviving accounts of the final outcome of the charges leveled against Patrick or of whether, as tradition has it, he stayed on in Ireland for the remainder of his days and never saw his home in Britain again.

The story of Patrick's death was not recorded until more than a hundred years after the fact, at a time when he had already achieved great prominence in his adopted homeland. Consequently, the accounts of his last days are filled with miraculous imagery reminiscent of the Old Testament, including heavenly visitations and even a burning bush. By this time, however, the location of Patrick's burial had been forgotten, leaving Ireland without the all-important relics of its patron saint or the chance to erect an elaborate sepulcher to mark his final resting place.

But perhaps the most fitting shrine to Patrick, given his self-effacing character, is simply the success of his life's work. His successors would take the Irish church in new directions. During the latter half of the first millennium, Christian clerics—not just in Ireland but throughout Europe—would increasingly turn inward, hoping to get close to God by shutting out the distractions and temptations of everyday life. In the words of one Irish monk, dedication to God required "stripping oneself of all the desires and possessions which bind a man to the present world."

In the monasteries that sprang up all over Ireland, monks could devote themselves to lives of study, work, and prayer. Some noble families donated their estates for the founding of monasteries, setting up their own kin as abbots. Additionally, Irish monks ventured abroad to establish outposts of Christianity among the peoples of continental Europe and Scotland, where there were still pagans to be converted.

In fact, the monastic system became so ingrained in the Irish church hierarchy that, in contrast to the rest of Europe, its abbots were often as powerful as bishops. An eighth-century English historian named Bede, describing an offshore Irish monastery, wrote "this island has an abbot for its ruler, who is a priest, to whose authority the whole province, including its bishops, are subject—

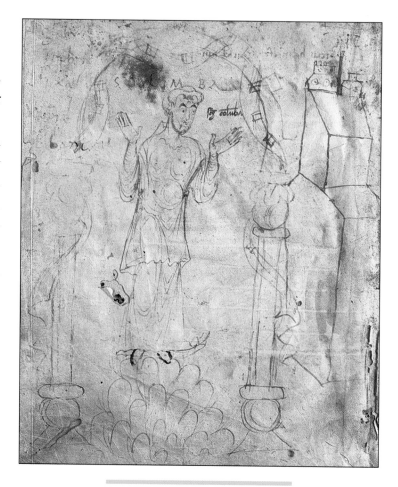

Columba rises miraculously to heaven in this pen-and-ink drawing from a seventh-century biography of the saint.

an unusual order of things in which they follow the example of their first teacher, who was not a bishop, but a priest and monk."

The monastery Bede described lay on the tiny island of Iona in the Hebrides chain off the west coast of Scotland. Its "first teacher" and founder was a man born three generations after Patrick went to Ireland and who, like his remarkable predecessor, was eventually destined for sainthood. His name was Columba.

Dermot felt his way carefully through the darkness of the courtyard. It was March in the year 576, and he shivered in the predawn chill. As always, he reached the door to his master's cell just as the first faint streaks of light illuminated the sky behind the black outline of the wooden church. The cell was a small wattle-and-daub structure with a narrow entranceway. Lighting a candle and stooping down, he went inside.

In the flickering shadows cast by the solitary flame, he made out the figure of a man lying on the rock floor, his head resting on a stone pillow. Gently, so as not to startle his master, Dermot placed his hand upon the sleeping man's shoulder. Columba stirred and slowly opened his eyes. He sat up, trying to stretch the stiffness and cold from his bones. Finally fully awake, he rose to his feet and slipped on a pair of leather shoes, brushed the dust from his ankle-length, white linen robe, and fastened a leather belt around his waist.

Dermot moved to a cupboard standing against the wall of the cell and poured water from a pitcher into a shallow wooden bowl. Columba dipped his hands into the ice-cold water and splashed it on his face, then stood motionless as his servant scraped at the stubble on his cheeks with an iron blade. This was the extent of his morning ablution; Columba was now ready to begin his daily duties as abbot of the monastery of Iona.

Dermot draped a woolen cloak around his master's shoulders, and the two men headed across the courtyard to the monastery's spiritual heart, the so-called oak house. This small, rectangular building served as the house of worship for Iona's 30 or so monks. They entered the church, then Dermot returned with a hand bell he rang vigorously, calling the monks to morning prayer.

By ones and twos the monks emerged from their cells into the dawn and made their way silently to the church. They were dressed in attire similar to that of their abbot, and all displayed what was called the Celtic tonsure—the top of the head was shaved forward of a line running from ear to ear with the hair growing long in the back. Filing

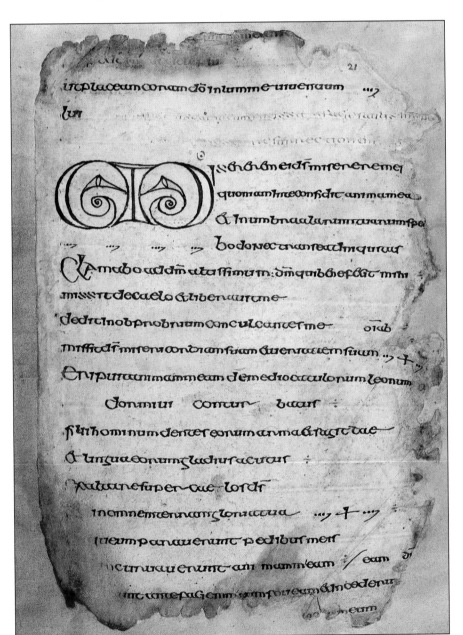

This page is from the *Cathach,* a copy of the Book of Psalms that may have been written in Columba's own hand. It dates from the sixth century and is the oldest Irish manuscript known.

DRAWING NEARER TO GOD

Eight miles off the southwestern coast of Ireland lies an island known as Skellig Michael *(far left)*, a bare pyramid of rock that rises 700 feet out of the Atlantic Ocean. A narrow stone stairway winds its way around the island, and near the top, six beehive-shaped huts *(near left)*, two oratories, and a church still mark the site of a small monastery that was inhabited for at least 500 years.

The monks who lived at Skellig Michael and at other remote places in Ireland sought to purify themselves through penance and prayer. Such a life could not have been easy, but at least one 12th-century Irish poet found joy in it. "Delightful I think it to be in the bosom of an isle, on the peak of a rock, that I might often see there the calm of the sea," he wrote. "That I might bless the Lord who has power over all, Heaven with its pure host of angels, earth, ebb, flood-tide."

down the aisle, they seated themselves on the hard wooden pews and began their daily meditation. As they did so, some might also have taken a moment to reflect on their abbot, whose indomitable presence had brought them—of their own free will—to this island community on the edge of the Atlantic Ocean.

By any measure, the abbot of Iona was an exceptional man. Born into the highest aristocratic circles of Irish society, he combined a natural aura of authority with a common touch that extended to all around him. His monks adored him, and it was said that even the monastery's animals responded to the power of his personality.

Like Patrick, Columba had several reverential biographers. Among them was Adomnán, the ninth abbot to succeed him at the Iona monastery. And like Patrick's biographers, Adomnán filled his writings with miraculous tales of his patron saint. But because written records were then better kept than in Patrick's day, there is more that can be said with certainty about the factual aspects of Columba's life.

Columba was born in the northern province of Ulster around the year 520 to an influential noble family and was a blood relative, in fact, of Loégaire, who had been king of Tara more than a century before. As was the custom among Irish royalty at that time, he was sent at a tender age to be raised by a foster father, a priest under whom he began his religious training. Later Columba became a deacon and studied scripture and "divine wisdom" at a church school in order to enter the priesthood himself. He was ordained in 551.

And then in 563, wrote Adomnán, Columba "sailed away from Ireland to Britain choosing to be a pilgrim for Christ." There are conflicting reports as to why he left his homeland. He may have been caught up in the political intrigue and blood feuds between his highborn kinsmen and other royal families. Some claim that Columba, like Patrick, had trouble with his ecclesiastical superiors and was brought before a church court on trumped-up charges. There is even a picturesque, if dubious, account of Columba in a battle against his family's enemies in which his prayers dissolved a mist created by druids to shroud the opposing army.

Whatever the reason, Columba and a small band of friends and relatives—Adomnán referred to them as Columba's 12 disciples—traveled northward away from their homeland and began to spread the word of God to the inhabitants of Scotland. According to the historian Bede, "he converted that people to the faith of Christ by his preaching and example, and received from them the island of Iona on which to found a monastery."

In this portrait from the *Book of Kells,* Saint John is shown with the traditional tools of a scribe—a quill pen and, below it, a small, cone-shaped inkpot.

spreading the gospel

All these things must have been the result of work not of man but of angels." So declared Gerald of Wales of a manuscript he saw in Kildare in 1185. The name of the book that provoked such praise is not known, but it was probably one of the painted gospel books made by Irish monks between the seventh and ninth centuries. The books were decorated with miniature pictures and elaborate designs such as spirals, geometric patterns, and interlaced ribbons and animals. If, as has been suggested, Gerald was examining the greatest illuminated manuscript of them all, the *Book of Kells*, the Welshman's reaction can easily be understood.

To produce these gospel books, which were copied onto specially prepared calfskin, monastic scribes and artists had an array of instruments and tools to call upon. They used reeds and the quills of geese, crows, and other birds, cut to a chisel point, to make both thick and thin lines; animal-fur brushes of varying fineness; and knives for scraping away mistakes.

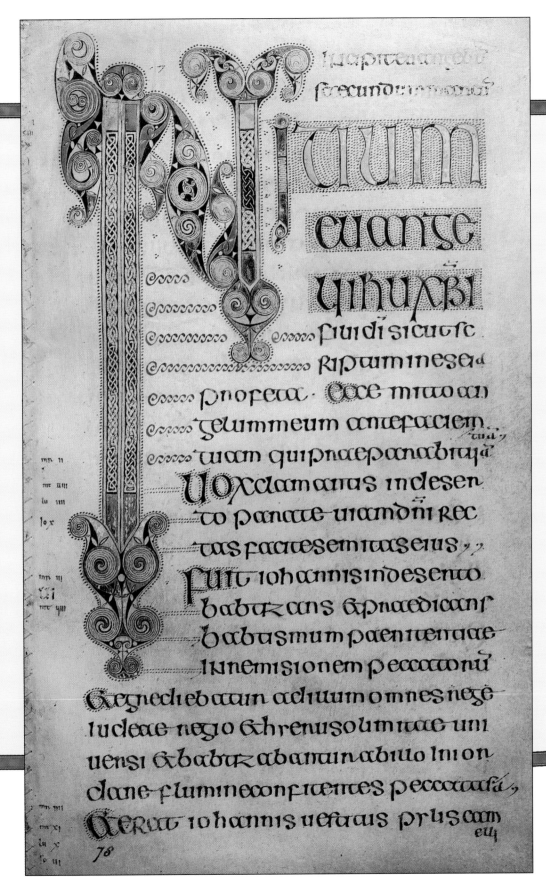

The Gospel of Mark in the *Book of Durrow* begins with an initial that incorporates two letters: the *I* and *N* of *Initium*, Latin for "the beginning."

Spirals, ribbons, and birds embellish the first letter of the Latin word for "inasmuch as," *Quoniam (below and inset),* in the Lindisfarne Gospel of Luke.

Cow-horn inkwells were stuck into the floor or attached to the arm of a scribe's chair, and ink was made from iron sulfate and crushed oak apples.

The great decorated pages, such as the ones introducing each of the four gospels, were designed with wooden compasses, rulers, and templates. For color, artists used plant and mineral pigments, some native to Ireland, while others—such as lapis lazuli from the Hindu Kush mountains of Afghanistan—were imported at great expense. One kind of red was made from a Mediterranean insect that fed only on a certain type of oak tree.

For all their beauty, the Irish gospel books had a practical purpose: the conversion of pagans. Many of the books were written in a large, clear script that was easy to read aloud in church, and the beautiful embellishments could be appreciated by illiterate congregations when the books were displayed on the altar or held aloft by a priest. More than a millennium later, we still look with awe at these masterpieces that invite us, as they did Gerald of Wales, to "penetrate with your eyes the secrets of the artistry."

To protect their precious books while traveling around the country, Irish missionaries carried them in leather satchels like this one.

Between the lines of Matthew's gospel in the *Book of Kells,* a striped cat watches a rat run off with what appears to be the communion bread.

"My hand is weary with writing;
my sharp great point is not thick;
my slender-beaked pen juts forth
a beetle-hued draught of bright blue ink.
I send my little dripping pen
unceasingly over an assemblage of
books of great beauty, to enrich the
possessions of men of art—whence my
hand is weary with writing."

Irish traditional,
11th century

A number of the monks who watched their beloved abbot in the oak house that chilly March morning could remember coming to Iona with Columba during the region's brief period of summerlike weather. Soon after their arrival they had set about building their compound on the eastern, leeward end of the small, uninhabited island. Stone was plentiful, but there were few trees on Iona, and to build their church, the monks had to tow pine and oak logs behind small skiffs across open water from the mainland. With insufficient time to prepare the rocky soil, plant crops, and gather a harvest before the onset of bad weather, the monks must have been dependent on supply ships from Ireland or Britain to help them get through the first winter on the island.

The next spring, however, they had embarked on the task of making their community self-sufficient. On a tract of arable land at the western end of the island, the monks had planted barley, then built stone enclosures around the fields as protection against the fierce, unceasing winds off the Atlantic. They brought in by boat a few cattle—and probably pigs and sheep—to provide meat and dairy goods.

Many more logs had been needed to build grain storehouses, barns, and fencing. Around the main courtyard containing the church and the monks' cells, guest quarters were added, and a kitchen was constructed a short distance apart from the other buildings because of the danger of fire. A small area in the courtyard was set aside for growing medicinal herbs. The monks also built an earthen bank that enclosed some 20 acres and marked the boundary of the monastery proper.

By the year 574 the monastic community was established, and soon it was attracting new initiates, not only Irish but Britons as well. With the construction work completed, the monks started to devote themselves to specialized labor: Some tilled the fields or tended the herds, while others became craftsmen—smiths, masons, or carpenters—to keep Iona's daily operations functioning smoothly.

The monks even built their own small fleet of both wood-planked and hide-covered boats for transportation and fishing. And though it would have been easy to find monks who were skilled as sailors and fishermen, the

rough seas and unpredictable weather of the Scottish coast still took their toll. One entry in the monastery's annals recalls a gale that "caused some six men of the community of Iona to drown."

As the island settlement grew, Columba was able to relieve some of his monks of their more mundane chores and assign them the task of copying manuscripts. This was a prestigious assignment, and the title of *scriba* was a badge of honor in the monastic world. It took a great deal of training in the art of calligraphy, and countless hours hunched over a desk in the dim light of his cell, for a scribe to produce one of the exquisite, illustrated volumes for which Irish monks are famed.

No matter what their position in the monastery, however, the life that the monks of Iona had chosen for themselves was a demanding one. Except for Sunday, which was given over completely to prayer, they devoted most of their waking hours

Discovered at a monastic site in southwestern Ireland in 1980, this cache of silver church vessels may have been hidden during a Viking raid.

to their labors; the rest of their time was spent at prayer or at meals.

At least the monks had nourishing and plentiful fare to keep up their strength. Barley—baked into loaves or ground up to make gruel—formed the staple of their diet. In summer, this was supplemented by onions, carrots, cabbage, peas, and beans, which were grown in garden plots. Cheese and butter were provided by dairy cows. Meat was saved for special occasions, but fish and oysters from the surrounding waters were always plentiful.

The monks drank water, milk, whey, and beer, although a few of the more rigid Irish monasteries forbade the consumption of alcohol. One anecdote from a slightly later period relates a conversation between two abbots: "The drink of forgetfulness of God shall not be drunk here," said one. To this the other replied, "Well, my household shall drink it, and they will be in heaven along with your household." But even the monasteries where beer was not imbibed would have brewed it on the premises to serve to guests.

The abbot of one Irish monastery known for its strictness summed up a monk's daily regimen this way: "Let him not do as he wishes, let him eat what he is bidden," he counseled. "Let him come weary to his bed and sleep walking, and let him be forced to rise while his sleep is not yet finished. Let him keep silence when he has suffered wrong, let him fear the superior of his community as a lord, love him as a father, believe that whatever he commands is healthful for himself, and let him not pass judgment on the opinion of an elder." By all accounts, Columba was more temperate with his monks than this particular abbot; they gladly carried out their superior's orders, not from fear of punishment, but out of boundless respect for the man.

In time, the reputation of the Iona monastery and its founder would spread far and wide, and Columba's original companions who had sailed with him from Ireland began establishing branch monasteries at other locations in the Hebrides and on the Scottish mainland, as well as back in Ireland. Soon Iona's isolation was a thing of the past; the island became the hub of an elaborate network of sea and land routes that linked the monks to the political and ecclesiastical centers of Ireland and Britain. Columba, in spite of his earlier troubles at home, had become a well-known and respected abbot, and he regularly sent envoys to kings and clerics alike. By the same token, a steady stream of visitors to Iona kept him in touch with family, friends, and the monasteries he had founded back in Ireland.

The gracious reception of guests was a hallmark of the Irish monastic tradition. Indeed, the welcome extended to any stranger coming ashore on Iona was about the only time the daily routine of the monastery was interrupted. The monks would often gather at the water's edge to greet the new arrival and offer a prayer of thanksgiving for the safe completion of his journey. Then they would lead their visitor to his quarters—much more comfortable than their own spartan cells—wash his feet, and attend to his every need. Although Wednesday and Friday were normally days of fasting, if a guest arrived on one of those days, the fast would be broken and a special meal, perhaps with meat, would be served. And most visitors, no matter what their station in life, probably received an audience with the island's famed abbot.

Columba would lead a long, productive life managing his string of monasteries and directing the day-to-day operations on Iona. At the age of 71, in fact, he was still assisting with the daily chores by carrying sacks of flour from the mill to the kitchen. Then one day about two years later, according to the biographer Adomnán, Columba had a vision of his approaching death. Two of his monks were conversing with him in his cell when suddenly his face took on an expression of "marvelous, blissful joy." But barely a moment later his look "turned to sad distress." The monks were sorely frightened and begged him to explain the vision that had caused such a profound change in his spirits.

Columba, overcome with emotion, made them promise not to tell a soul. Then, with tears streaming down his cheeks, he

terror from the seas

Although Ireland's conversion to Christianity was remarkably peaceful, a threat to the new religion emerged by the end of the eighth century. The threat came in the form of seaborne raiders from Scandinavia, variously referred to as Danes, Norsemen, or, simply, "the foreigners." We know them today as Vikings.

At first the raids were sporadic, targeting vulnerable coastal monasteries. But by the 820s Viking forces were sailing up the Boyne, Liffey, and Shannon Rivers into the heart of Ireland. Although the Irish fought back with some success, they failed to discourage the invaders, who carried off valuable metalwork and captives for the slave market. A monk described a rare night without dread: "Bitter is the wind tonight, / It tosses the ocean's white hair; / Tonight I fear not the fierce warriors of Norway, / Coursing on the Irish Sea."

Typically, the Vikings launched their attacks and then withdrew, but in 839 they overwintered on Lough Neagh. Two years later they founded permanent camps on the Liffey that one day would become the city of Dublin. The Vikings—soon to adopt Christianity themselves—had come to stay.

The Vikings braved rocky coasts like the one above to attack Irish monasteries. The stone figures at right are from a monument recalling a raid on Lindisfarne in 793.

"Immense floods and countless sea-vomitings of ships and boats and fleets so that there was not a harbor nor a land-port nor a dun nor a fortress nor a fastness in all Mumhan [Munster] without floods of Danes and pirates . . . so that they made spoil-land and sword-land and conquered land of her, throughout her breadth and generally; and they ravaged her chieftainries and her privileged churches and her sanctuaries; and they rent her shrines and her reliquaries and her books."

Wars of the Irish with the Foreigners, 12th century

commenced: "Today is the thirtieth anniversary since I began to live in pilgrimage in Britain. A long time ago I earnestly asked the Lord that at the end of this thirtieth year he would release me from this dwelling and call me straightaway to the heavenly kingdom." He had appeared joyful, he explained, because "I saw the angels sent from the throne on high to lead my soul from this body. But see, now they are suddenly delayed, and wait standing on a rock across our island Sound. . . . Though the Lord had granted what I desired," he went on, "none the less he has answered the prayers of many churches concerning me. For these churches have prayed the Lord that, even though I do not want it, four years longer must I remain in this flesh."

The abbot's vision would indeed come true. One day in the spring of his 77th year, Columba asked for a cart to drive him to the western end of Iona. There he addressed the monks working in the fields. "At Easter in the month of April just past, I longed deeply to depart to Christ the Lord," he told them. "But so as not to make the festival of gladness into one of sorrow for you, I preferred to put off a little longer the day of my departure from the world." The monks were aghast to hear these words from their abbot, and Columba stayed with them awhile to console them as best he could. Then, with their grief-stricken eyes following him, he made his way back to the monastery.

A few days later during Sunday Mass, Columba had a vision of an angel descending into the church to collect the "loan" of his soul; he knew his time was drawing near. The next week he spent making the rounds with his faithful servant, Dermot, to satisfy himself that the grain silos were well stocked and that all the monastery's workshops were running smoothly.

During one of these tours, a workhorse, used to haul milk pails from the island's dairy farm, came down the

SACRED STONES

Reminiscent of an ancient pagan fertility symbol, a standing stone inscribed with a cross *(left)* bears testimony to the way the Irish blended Christianity with their ancestral beliefs. Later, following the same tradition, Irish high crosses created out of a single slab of stone began to dot the landscape.

The high cross at right stands in the cemetery of the Clonmacnoise monastery on the banks of the Shannon and is an example of the type known as a scripture cross. Carved on all its sides are scenes from the Old and New Testaments. Scripture crosses helped missionaries spread the gospel to an illiterate populace and were, perhaps, a symbol of the Christian faith meant for Viking invaders.

The round tower in the background may have sheltered monks and their treasures from the raiding Norsemen. The monks could enter the tower by climbing a ladder up to the high doorway and then draw the ladder up after themselves.

path and stopped in front of Columba. The horse tenderly lowered its head and—in the words of Adomnán—"began to mourn like a person, pouring out its tears in the saint's bosom and weeping aloud with foaming lips."

Columba blessed the animal, then turned and climbed a small nearby hill that overlooked the monastery. Gazing out over the tightly knit community that had been home for most of his adult life, he raised his hands and declared: "This place, however small and mean, will have bestowed on it no small but great honour by the kings and peoples of Ireland, and also by the rulers of even barbarous and foreign nations with their subject tribes. And the saints of other churches too will give it great reverence."

Then, in the late afternoon light, the ab-

There is a story in Adomnán's book of a conversation that took place years before Columba's death. "When you are dead," one of the monks is said to have remarked to the abbot, "it is reckoned that all the population of these provinces will row here and fill the whole island of Iona to attend your funeral ceremonies." To this Columba calmly replied that when the time came, his funeral would be attended only by the monks of his own community.

Again Columba's prophecy would come true. Soon after he died a great storm blew up and raged for three days and nights, preventing anyone on the mainland from reaching Iona. Thus it was left to his own monks to conduct the funeral services, wrap his body in a shroud of pure linen, and lay their beloved abbot in his grave. And in an altogether proper conclusion to the story,

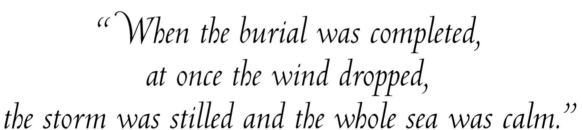

> "When the burial was completed,
> at once the wind dropped,
> the storm was stilled and the whole sea was calm."

bot returned to his cell to continue one of his current tasks, writing out a copy of the Psalms. That night as the bell rang for midnight Mass, he hurried from his cell and entered the darkened church ahead of the other monks. "Father, where are you?" cried out Dermot, following behind. Feeling his way up the aisle, he found Columba lying before the altar. The other monks rushed in carrying lamps and gathered around his prostrate form. Cradling his dying master in his arms, Dermot held up Columba's right arm so that he might give one final blessing to the monks. "Then at once," in the words of Adomnán, "he gave up the ghost." Columba's body was reverently carried back to his cell and his head placed gently on the stone pillow.

Adomnán says that "when the burial was completed, at once the wind dropped, the storm was stilled and the whole sea was calm. This then was the end of our praiseworthy patron's life and the beginning of his rewards."

Ireland had undergone tremendous changes in the hundred or so years between Loégaire, the pagan king, and Columba, the Irish saint. In the centuries ahead, the winds of change would continue to blow, bringing foreign influences and ideas to this distant corner of Europe. But the new could never fully replace the old. Like Lugh, Núadha, and the Túatha Dé Danaan, the ghosts of the past would be immortalized in Irish myth, and part of Ireland would remain forever true to the island's Celtic soul.

the pilgrims' progress

As Christianity took hold in Ireland, many felt called to set out on pilgrimage. Following the example set by such visionaries as Patrick and Columba, missionaries, royalty, and common folk alike left their homeland and went in great numbers to the Continent to gain their place in heaven by leading lives of poverty, hardship, and penance. By the ninth century, the number of Irish *peregrini,* or pilgrims, wandering in Europe was so large that the German monk Walafrid Strabo referred to them as "the Irish people with whom the custom of travelling to foreign lands has now become almost second nature."

The typical Irish pilgrim traveled light, wearing sturdy shoes and carrying only the hallmarks of pilgrimage, a bell and a walking staff, as shown in the eighth- or ninth-century stone carving at left. Eventually, restrictions imposed by the established Continental churches on poor and homeless wanderers as well as the dangers posed by recurrent Viking raids caused the Irish faithful to confine their travels to sacred sites within their own borders. In traveling to the places made holy by saints such as Brigit, Brendan, Kevin, and Patrick, the pilgrims also, perhaps unknowingly, paid tribute to spots long associated with the pagan gods Ireland had abandoned centuries before.

Pilgrims seeking blessings from Saint Brigit *(above)* visited holy wells such as this one in Mullingar *(left)* that bears both her name and her distinctive cross. In pagan times springs and wells were considered entrances to the hidden world of the gods. The wells that later came under the protection of Saint Brigit were believed to cure sterility and other ailments.

BRIGIT, IRELAND'S GODDESS-SAINT

More than any other Irish saint, Brigit represents Ireland's transition from paganism to Christianity. The daughter of a noble pagan father and a Christian slave woman who by some accounts worked for a druid, Brigit, according to legend, blinded herself in one eye so that she would be unmarriageable—and thus able to devote herself completely to God. Although some scholars question whether a historical Brigit ever existed, she is second only to Saint Patrick in the devotion of her followers.

Many of Saint Brigit's qualities can be traced to an older Brigit, a goddess of the Celtic pantheon who was a daughter of the Dagdha, or "good god," and patroness of livestock. The pagan Imbolc festival, held annually on February 1, honored Brigit's role in the birth of lambs and the lactation of ewes; Saint Brigit's feast day is also February 1. The biographers of the earthly Brigit ascribed to her many of the attributes of the fertility goddess, although they gave these qualities a distinctly Christian character. They describe Saint Brigit as a compassionate figure who was able to produce prodigious quantities of milk and butter for weary travelers and the poor. She transformed her bathwater into beer to slake the thirst of visiting clerics and, one Easter Sunday, made enough ale from one measure of malt to serve 17 churches in County Meath.

Stories about her life credit Saint Brigit with founding a monastery in Kildare sometime during the fifth century. It was Ireland's first religious community for women, and it transformed a powerful pagan site into a center of Christian worship. The name Kildare derives from the Irish "Cell Dara," or "church of the oak," a tree sacred to the druids. The monastery was home to an eternal flame that burned originally in honor of the goddess Brigit but was tended by 19 nuns in the name of Saint Brigit until the year 1220, when church fathers stopped the practice.

A 16th-century reliquary shaped like a slipper *(below)* is said to have held the shoe of Saint Brigit; her cross adorns a metal cup *(left)* resting beside a holy well.

salnt brendan's voyage

Before his retreat on the Dingle Peninsula on Ireland's southwest coast *(opposite)* became a favored destination for Irish pilgrims, Saint Brendan was himself a pilgrim. As the story goes, in the sixth century Brendan and 17 monks set off in a coracle, a round-bottomed, hide-covered boat, to traverse the "western seas" in search of the Promised Land of the Saints. For seven years they sailed to one fantastic island after another. Once they stopped on an island bare of rocks or vegetation and lighted a cooking fire with driftwood. When the ground began to tremble beneath them, they hastily retreated—to find that they had put ashore on a whale's back.

Saint Brendan and his crew eventually returned safely to Ireland to found a monastery at Clonfert in County Galway. In the centuries that followed, pilgrims emulated the saint by making seaborne pilgrimages of their own to the islands off the Irish coast. An important stop along the way was Saint Brendan's Seat, the point atop Mount Brandon on the Dingle Peninsula *(opposite, far right)* where the saint is said to have built the boat for his epic voyage.

Created more than 500 years before Brendan's voyage, this gold replica of a coracle *(below)* was outfitted with 18 oars—the number needed by the saint and his crew for their ocean journey.

Saint Brendan extends a blessing to a mermaid, one of many fantastic creatures he was said to have encountered on his seven-year voyage in the North Atlantic.

saint kevin's retreat

Unlike the accounts of the lives of some of Ireland's saints, Saint Kevin's biography suggests that he preferred a life of calm piety and monastic seclusion. Little is known of his origins; it is believed that he was born of a noble Leinster family that had fallen out of favor with the royal house. After being educated by monks, Kevin was ordained. He then set out to live as a hermit in Glendalough, County Wicklow *(opposite)*, reportedly guided to a propitious spot by an angel. The cleric lived ascetically in a cave that came to be known as Saint Kevin's Bed; it is likely that the cave had once served as a tomb in the Bronze Age. As disciples began to gather around him, Kevin presided over the growing community, establishing churches and a monastery that gained renown for its scholarship.

The monastery at Glendalough eventually became one of the holiest shrines in Ireland—so revered that seven pilgrimages to its environs offered as many indulgences as one pilgrimage to Rome. Glendalough itself is a wonderfully beautiful and inspirational spot; it is the perfect setting for the home of a saint reputed to be in harmony with nature. It was said that the community of monks there was sustained for some time by salmon brought to Kevin by an otter and that the saint spent so peaceable a life that he lived until he was 120. But these stories of gentleness and empathy with other creatures contrast sharply with one showing Kevin to have a sterner side; according to this account, the saint threw from a cliff a woman who came to tempt him away from his life of pious contemplation.

A narrow slit in the wall of Glendalough's Reefert Church *(left)* allowed pilgrims seeking a relic just enough room to lower strips of cloth onto Saint Kevin's grave beyond the wall. A timeworn effigy of the saint *(right)* still adorns a 12th-century cross at Glendalough.

Saint Patrick, in the first etching at right, indicates the pit that Christ revealed to him, where a person could experience heaven and hell and be purged of all sin forever. In later years a pilgrim enters the pit to perform his penance as churchmen look on *(second panel)*.

In patrick's steps

The best-known of Ireland's holy men, Saint Patrick, has two often-visited sites associated with him, Croagh Patrick and Lough Derg. Pilgrimages to these sacred places, one strictly Christian and one with ancient origins, continue to the present day.

The mountain in County Mayo called Croagh Patrick *(opposite)* was once known as Cruachan Aigle and may have been a site where the pre-Christian Irish held summer festival rites in honor of the sun god, Lugh. Although Christian pilgrimages to Croagh Patrick are undertaken all year, the most popular time has always been the same as the pagan feast—the last Sunday of July. Traditionally, the pilgrims begin their ascent of the mountain at midnight, in their bare feet. With only a lamp or candle to light the way, the climb takes about three hours and culminates at a cairn that is called Mary's Cemetery but that resembles an ancient burial mound.

The pilgrims' ascent of Croagh Patrick follows in the tradition of the saint himself. Patrick was said to have climbed the mountain to fast and pray for 40 days and 40 nights. While there he was set upon by a flock of black birds—demons led by the devil's mother. He shook the bell *(right)* he always carried at them but failed to drive the birds away. He finally hurled the bell at them; hitting one, the bell turned from silver to iron.

Patrick fought the devil's mother again at Lough Derg (Red Lake), killing her and turning the waters red with her blood. But pilgrims today travel to Lough Derg to visit another of its features, a cave on the island there known as Saint Patrick's Purgatory *(above)*. There, it was said, the torments of hell could be witnessed firsthand, converting all who saw.

CHAPTER TWO

the rhythms of country life

Properly groomed Irishmen could choose from a variety of hair styles, but the facial hair they grew was governed by their social status. The wealthy either were clean shaven or wore both a beard and a mustache, like these figures from the *Book of Kells*. Soldiers and the poor wore long mustaches without any beard.

When Librán awoke that morning in late March, the first thing he realized was that it was quiet. All around him the other members of his family were still asleep. But it was another kind of silence Librán had noticed. Staring up into the darkness above him, he could tell that the characteristic patter on the roof's thick thatch was gone: It had stopped raining at last. Careful not to wake anyone, he rose from the straw pallet on which he had spent the night and crept outside. A dull gray light was just visible on the eastern horizon, and Librán made his way toward it.

A short walk brought him to the outer limit of his family's rath, the circular ring-fort that was his home. The boundary of the rath—which was about 100 feet in diameter—was marked by an earthen embankment and ditch that provided some protection against any wolves or thieves tempted by the cattle, pigs, and sheep penned up inside the ring-fort at night. After pausing to check on the animals, the young man climbed to the top of the low embankment.

Librán resembled most of his male compatriots. He was a sturdy-looking man with a beard and fair reddish hair that fell to his shoulders. He was dressed in normal everyday attire—knee-length linen

tunic cinched at the waist with a leather belt. Over this, to ward off any lingering winter chill, he wore a woolen cloak wrapped around him several times and fastened over his chest with a pin. These were the garments of early medieval Ireland, for women as well as men, and Librán probably had worn them for some time without benefit of bath.

As he gazed out over the Irish countryside in the growing light of dawn, Librán could see at a glance all that made up his world in this little corner of Connacht. Below him, drying now in the soft spring breeze and destined for grain and green vegetables, lay a cluster of small, fenced fields that fairly cried out for the plow. Farther off, a patchwork of forest and pasture land rolled to the horizon, beyond which stretched a variegated landscape of low mountains, extensive bogs, and heavy forest. Much of the land was kept green all year by the warmth of the Gulf Stream and by the nearly 50 inches of annual rainfall that manifested itself virtually every other day except in spring.

But, Librán reminded himself, the rain had stopped now. The lean days of winter—of eating salt pork and porridge—were over. For the past two months the livestock had been giving birth, and the cows, freshening with milk, gave promise of the butter and cheese that farmers called "summer food."

Yes, the busy time in the agricultural year was here again, and Librán's long workday was about to begin. Soon he would make his way back to the family home that sat in the middle of the ring-fort—a tiny round house no more than 20 feet wide, assembled from posts, wattle, and daub. But somehow it sheltered under its mop of wheat-colored thatch Librán's parents and his brothers and sisters, all of whom would be stirring now, as the household came to life.

Tucked into the verdant Irish landscape of 32,600 square miles were thousands of little worlds like Librán's. During the late sixth century AD, when the young man lived, Ireland consisted almost entirely of single rural farmsteads centered on circular ring-forts, many of them more prosperous than that of Librán's family but similar in their essential nature. The only settlements that remotely resembled towns were the small communities that were beginning to grow up around monasteries. Since roads were primitive and travel by land difficult, people rarely ventured far from their own farms and almost never beyond their local district.

But no matter how isolated, the inhabitants of these scattered farmsteads were bound in a closely knit and rigidly stratified society held together by ties of kinship and strong interpersonal links. Tradition and custom rather than government dictated these rela-

Although most farmers lived in ring-forts, some built fortified artificial islands like this one, called crannogs.

tionships, preserved order, and provided models of acceptable behavior. Moreover, everyday life was regulated by an extraordinarily detailed complex of rights and obligations originating in oral tradition and codified in the voluminous law tracts compiled by jurists, many of whom were monks.

Librán's father was known as an *ócaire,* or small farmer. According to the law tracts, an ócaire's possessions amounted to four acres, seven cows, one bull, seven pigs, seven sheep, and a horse. Librán and his brothers belonged to the legal category called "sons of a living father." Until their father died and they received their inheritance of land, they were considered dependents, subject to the authority of their father.

The nuclear family formed by Librán, his parents, brothers, and sisters was part of a larger kinship group called the *fine.* This group represented four generations of male kinsmen, typically including all male descendants of a common great-grandfather. The fine was the basic landholding unit in the Irish economy. The fields near Librán's home, for example, were owned and largely controlled by the fine, which had to rule on such matters as the sale of any parcel of the land. The fine acted also as a pressure group to ensure that its members met their legal obligations.

The rules governing inheritance declared that upon his death, Librán's father's share of the land would pass to his sons. In order to guarantee that each heir received a share of equal value, the youngest son normally would divide the property, and his brothers would then select their portions, with the oldest son choosing first. Since the youngest chose last, it was in his interest to make as equitable a division as possible.

Standing on the boundary of the family ring-fort that March morning, Librán knew that while he and his brothers would one day inherit parcels of their own, for the present they had to team up to help their father. And in common with everyone else in rural Ireland, great or small, their daily lives revolved around the cycle of the seasons. It had, reflected Librán, been a long year.

For Librán and his family, the seasonal round had begun with the breaking of ground the previous March, as soon as the soil was sufficiently dry. Like most ócaires, his father would have cultivated several small fields, each fenced in with piled-up stones or with upright posts connected by interwoven branches and crested by prickly blackthorn to keep out the livestock. In the fall, after the growing season, the fields would have been prepared for the next year by turning the cows out to graze on the harvest stubble and spread their manure. Additional nutrients for the soil came from seaweed, if available, and ashes from wood fires or, in the case of new ground, from burning the covering turf.

The plowing itself called for a cooperative effort. Since Librán's father himself could not afford to maintain a complete plowing outfit—or the four oxen it required—he pooled resources with three of his neighboring kinsmen. The four farmers jointly owned the plow, which probably was one of the comparatively recent models with an iron colter, or knife, mounted vertically in front of the iron-shod plowshare. The colter sliced through matted roots and the heavy, moisture-laden soil, enabling the share to create a deeper furrow than had been possible with the older, lighter plows.

The iron parts for the plow would have been fashioned by the local blacksmith, an important figure in Irish society and one who was often regarded as possessing supernatural powers. According to one legal text, "the moulding-block of a blacksmith" was one of "the three renovators of the world," the other two being "the womb of a woman" and "the udder of a cow."

After plowing deep furrows and then harrowing with a thornbush to break up the larger clods of earth, the men began planting. Librán's family had sown the fields in grain—primarily barley but also oats and rye—and a variety of vegetables. The vegetables would have included onions, peas, beans, cabbages, parsnips, and carrots.

This fine bronze cauldron and flesh fork for piercing meat, ornamented with water birds, date to the early seventh and eighth centuries BC. By medieval times, every substantial farmer in Ireland was expected to own a cauldron and a spit on which beef, pork, or mutton could be cooked.

But while crops were greatly valued, it was the cow that sustained the family and the Irish economy. In addition to meat, milk, butter, and cheese, cattle yielded a versatile hide from which could be fashioned shoes, harnesses, buckets, and boats. And from calfskin came the vellum upon which monks copied the Scriptures as well as the great turbulent sagas and the laws that governed everyday life. Indeed, the cow was so central to the economy that, in the absence of money, it served as a standard unit of value—one *sét* equaling half a milk cow. The importance of cows was further attested to by a coming-of-age ritual popular among young noblemen, who were called upon by tradition to demonstrate their manhood in the art of stealing cows. Such raids gave rise to an entire genre in Irish literature—that of the *táin,* or cattle raid.

Shortly after May 1, when they celebrated Beltane, the festival that marked the official beginning of the Irish summer, Librán and his family moved their cows and sheep to communal summer pasture in the mountains. This transfer, known as *booleying,* got the stock away from the newly cultivated fields and permitted them to graze on fresh upland grass while the pastures near home recovered to provide feed during the winter. If the herd

By the 14th century, after several waves of Celtic migration from Europe, a succession of tribal wars and displacements, and invasion by the Vikings and Anglo-Normans, the great families of Ireland had settled in these territories.

what's in a name?

According to tradition, when the Celts invaded Ireland from continental Europe, the Irish goddess Ériu quickly bestowed her blessing upon the new arrivals. "Yours shall be this island for ever," the goddess declared, "and to the east of the world there shall not be a better island." In response the Celts agreed to name the land for her, and so it became Ériu, Eire, and eventually, Ireland. The names of Ireland's people and places likewise spring from both native Celtic traditions and the influence of newcomers to the island: Christian, Viking, and Anglo-Norman.

Many of the oldest placenames of Ireland are descriptive of local landscape features, incorporating words such as *drum*, meaning a height, as in Drumbeg; *knock*, a hill, as in Knocknagoney; or *derry*, oak woods, as in Derryaghy. Later, terms for man-made features were added, such as *rath*, denoting a fort, as in Rathcoole; or *bally*, a farm, as in Ballymacarrett. And later still, the names of clans and prominent people were used to designate specific sites. But nothing influenced the evolution of placenames more than Christianity. Many a mountain, island, and spring bears the name of a native saint, and two of the most common prefixes, *kill*, as in Kil-

Known as the Gríanán of Ailech, this stone fort was the chief seat of the northern line of the powerful O'Neill dynasty. The fort is located on a hilltop between two valleys near the modern-day city of Londonderry, and like many ancient Irish names, *gríanán* is descriptive, meaning "sunny place."

IRISH SURNAMES AND THEIR SOURCES

Many of today's most-common Irish surnames date back to the island's ancient families and reflect the variety of cultural and religious factors at play in Celtic Ireland. The names below are given in both their Anglicized and Irish forms, along with their historical origins or meaning.

NAME IN ENGLISH	NAME IN IRISH	HISTORY/DERIVATION
Burke (Bourke, de Burgh)		among the most powerful Norman settlers, the Burkes descended from William Fitz Adelm de Burgo, a Norman knight
Cleary (O'Cleary, Clark)	Ó Cléirigh	perhaps the oldest European surname, from *cléirech*, meaning "cleric" or "scribe"; the early bearers were renowned for their works on Irish history
Daly (Daily, O'Daley)	Ó Dálaigh	from *dálach*, "one who is present at assemblies"; the name derives from a learned family of scholars and poets
Farrell (Ferrell, O'Farrell)	Fearghail	from a personal name meaning "man of valor"
Fitzpatrick (Kilpatrick, Gilpatrick)	Mac Giolla Phádraiga	Norman rendering of the Irish for "son of the follower of Patrick"
Flynn (O'Flynn, Lynn)	Ó Floinn	from *flann*, which means "reddish" or "ruddy" and was a common personal name
Hennessy (O'Hennessy)	Ó hAonghasa	from the name Angus, or Óengus, the pagan Celtic god said to reside at Newgrange
Kavanagh (Cavanagh, Cavanaugh)	Coemgen	one of the few Irish surnames without O or Mac, it designates a "follower of Saint Kevin"
Kennedy (O'Kennedy)	Ó Cennétig	meaning "ugly-headed" or "rough-headed," the name originated with the father of King Brian Boru
Leary (O'Leary)	Ó Loégaire	from a name meaning "cattle lord," no doubt a reference to the ancestor's trade; the family became a maritime power
MacBride (Kilbride, Gilbride)	Mac Giolla Bhrighde	the Irish means "son of the follower of Saint Brigit"; among the original bearers of the name were many ecclesiastics
MacCarthy	Mac Cárthaigh	from *cárthach*, "loving"; the name is primarily associated with the chief family of the tribal group the Eóganacht
MacLoughlin (McLaughlin)	Mac Lochlainn	from *loch*, meaning "lake" or "fjord"; a name applied to Norway and sometimes Scandinavia generally; also associated with a branch of the O'Neill tribe in the 12th century
Maguire (MacGuire)	Mag Uidhir	meaning "son of the brown-haired one," it was borne by a line of distinguished soldiers and church officials
O'Brien (O'Brian)	Ó Briain	may derive from the Irish for "eminent"; used in the 11th and 12th centuries to designate a descendant of Brian Boru
O'Neill (O'Neal)	Ó Néill	from the personal name Niall, which may mean "vehement"; the Uí Neill were the most important dynastic group in Ireland throughout most of the pre-Norman period
O'Toole (Toole)	Ó Tuathail	from a personal name meaning "ruler of the people"
Quinn (O'Quin)	Ó Coinn	among the 20 most-common surnames in Ireland, it derives from a personal name meaning "chief" or "leader"
Scott		from the Latin *Scottus*, meaning "Irishman"
Ward	Mac an Bháird	meaning "son of the bard or poet," the name is common throughout Ireland

lyleagh, and *donagh,* as in Donaghadee, come from Irish words for "church."

Christianity also introduced many new Irish personal names. The prefix *Gil-,* for example, is an Anglicized form of *gilla,* Irish for "follower" or "servant." Thus, "MacGillycuddy" translates as "son of the follower of Saint Mochuda." Also common was *Mul-,* from *máel,* the Irish word for "bald," alluding to the grooming of monks. Thus, a Mulligan or a Moloney probably descended from a "servant of the church."

Other personal names derived from physical characteristics. The popular name Flann, for instance, means "ruddy," while Finn denotes "fair haired" and Cassidy "curly headed." Allusions to personal traits or livelihoods also frequently appear, as in Conall, which translates as "strong as a wolf," or Murphy, "sea warrior."

To form surnames the Irish added the prefix *Mac,* meaning "son of," to the personal name of the father (or occasionally the name of the mother). Such surnames were not hereditary, however, lasting only one generation. Conchobar Mac Néill, for example, would have been Conchobar (or Connor) the son of Níall, while his son—Diarmait, say—would be Diarmait (or Dermot) Mac Conchobair. But in a land rife with clan rivalries, fixed surnames became a political necessity, and by the 11th century Irish families began to adopt truly hereditary names. They did this by maintaining, generation after generation, the personal name of an important ancestor and adding to it one of two prefixes, either *Mac* or *O,* the latter meaning "grandson of."

As Viking and Norman invaders settled down and adopted Irish ways, *Mac* was combined with Norse personal names, like Magnus, to produce Irish names, such as MacManus, "son of Magnus"; and *Fitz-,* a corruption of *fils,* the French word for "son," became the Norman version of *Mac.* Indeed, a large number of surnames that appear distinctly Irish have their origins in Normandy or other parts of France. Such names include Power, which comes from *le povre,* "the poor one"; Dillon, or de Leon, from Leon in Brittany; and Roche, originally de la Roche.

Irish names reflect the history of Ireland: Both are a product of the different peoples and influences that have made their way to the island over the millenniums, each changing in some way what existed before and each, in turn, changed by what was yet to come.

had to cross a neighbor's land to reach the distant pasture, the law provided access, but only under certain conditions: The crossing had to be properly witnessed and supervised by three kinsmen of the cattleman and three of the landowner.

In fact, the law tracts that had been set down by the monks spelled out in exhausting detail the damages for all kinds of trespass. There was even a provision for the way apples fell in the autumn. If apples from one neighbor's tree landed on the property of another, they shared the fruit for three years; only in the fourth year did the owner of the property on which the apples were falling have the right to gather all the fruit himself.

The cows that Librán's family took into the mountains in May were joined by the herds of their neighboring kinsmen. Like plowing, booleying was a cooperative endeavor. The kin group, or fine, used the same summer pastures, and some of the women and children of the fine would spend the summer there to guard the commingled herds against attacks by predators. The cows were highly productive during their first three months in summer pasture, each yielding up to three gallons of milk a day. During this period women from Librán's family probably went up there to milk, churn butter, and make hard and soft cheeses.

Meanwhile, most of the men cultivated and then harvested the crops. The harvest was a time of great anxiety. The rain that made the island green and lush virtually year round also tended to delay the harvest, which was constantly threatened with ruin. Librán and his brothers would have used sickles (the longer, more efficient scythe was not yet known in Ireland) to cut the grain just below the ear, leaving the stalk for later consumption by their cattle. But it was almost always so damp from August through October that before the grain could be threshed and milled into flour, it first had to be dried and hardened in a kiln. The kiln, probably owned jointly with several kinsmen, likely consisted of a pit layered with clay or stones and fired with peat. Small farmers probably stored the harvest in shared barns or in temporary structures made out of twigs, straw, and rope.

The herds returned from summer pasture in late October and were turned into nearby fields, from which they drew their winter sustenance. Because the grass grew throughout the year and the occasional snowfall seldom stayed long on the ground, Irish farmers did not cut and save hay to feed their cows during the winter. But to keep down the numbers feeding on the sparser winter grass, Librán's family would cull the herd, slaughtering the older cows and those male calves not needed for stud. They would then preserve the beef for winter by salting or curing it, using salt purchased at market or obtained by boiling seawater or burning seaweed. As the weather got colder, the pigs that had fattened on household scraps and the acorns, beechnuts, and chestnuts they found in the nearby woods would be butchered and converted into salt pork, sausage, and smoked bacon.

All this meat—"winter food"—would be sorely needed in the months ahead. After the festival of Samhain marked the beginning of winter on November 1, the family stayed indoors much of the time and prepared for the feast they had to give every year for the local lord and his retinue.

The lord was an important figure in the lives of small farmers like Librán's father. Many of the cows herded to the highlands had been rented to the family by a nobleman under an arrangement known as clientship. Clientship was the very bedrock of Irish society. So intrinsic was the institution, in fact, that while most other contracts were considered invalid if made when the parties had drunk too much alcohol, lord-

Many farmers were granted livestock and land by nobles in exchange for services and a share of the harvest; however, sometimes conflicts arose over loyalties, as may be illustrated in this picture of two men coming to blows.

client agreements were typically concluded by the consumption of great amounts of ale.

To satisfy a lord's grant of livestock (and possibly land), the client supplied him with labor and military service, together with stipulated annual amounts of bread, ale, honey, bacon, and other foods. The client also provided an obligatory annual night of hospitality for the lord and his entourage during the winter.

Again, Irish law tracts are specific about the extent of these obligations. A lord of the lowest rank, for example, was entitled to a night's hospitality for himself and up to four other guests; the highest-ranking lord, however, could expect food and drink for as many as a dozen. Written sources also prescribed what kinds of food should be offered and to whom: "the haunch for the king, bishop and senior man of learning; a leg for a young chief."

The visit of the lord was a time of considerable tension. Much of a family's respect and standing in the kin group depended on treating its guests appropriately. The lord could refuse the food if he found it "bitter or mawkish." And fines could be levied for an insensitive act by the host, such as lighting a candle after the lord had retired for the night; after all, reasoned one source, the light might startle him into thinking he was about to be assassinated.

Once their obligations as hosts had been fulfilled, Librán's family would have done what most other families did at this time of year. During the dark winter months, the Irish stayed mainly indoors, settling contracts and making marriage arrangements with neighboring families. It was a period for rest and socializing, a time when the people could again look forward to the more pleasant aspects of the annual round: the birth of new livestock, the cows coming in to milk, the start of spring plowing, and the promise of "summer food."

Like other young men of his acquaintance, Librán seemed destined to live out his years in rhythm with this Irish seasonal cycle. But as events turned out, before he could inherit his share of his father's land and begin life on his own as a small farmer, tragedy overtook him. The myriad rules and regulations through which Irish law attempted to hold back violence broke down—and Librán murdered a man. Perhaps he and the other man were drinking at a feast and argued about the status of their respective families, or they might

Drinking was an important social activity in early Ireland, where a man might be measured by his capacity to down ale. This wooden cup would have been passed around a group of friends, each of whom would take a drink from one of its corners.

have fought over the favors of a young woman. We do not know. The crime took place in his own native province of Connacht, but the circumstances were not otherwise explained by the abbot, Adomnán, who told Librán's story.

What happened next illustrates the peculiar nature of early Irish justice. Like criminals in many other societies, Librán was captured and placed in chains. However, this duty was not performed by officers of the public peace, for there were none. Nor did there exist a public jail in which he might be imprisoned. Rather, the men who shackled Librán were the kindred of his victim. Their kinship group, like all fines, took an active role in obtaining justice for any member who was wronged. They had the lawful right to hold Librán prisoner as a condemned person until an indemnity was paid by himself or by his kinsmen. And if that payment was not forthcoming, they could sell him into slavery or even execute him.

In early Ireland criminal law as we know it did not exist. All felonies and misdemeanors were considered civil offenses that could be redeemed by legally prescribed payments to the victim. In the case of murder, damages were to be paid to the victim's relatives. Payments for homicide were of two types: a "body price" of approximately 21 cows, and a further set of "honor prices" that were based on the status of the kinsmen and the closeness of their relationship with the victim. The penalty for murder could therefore be considerable. And if the murderer himself was unable to pay the price, his own kin group—the fine—was stuck with the bill.

In Librán's instance, his immediate family was too poor to pay the body price or the various honor prices for the murder he had committed. And his fine either could not or would not fulfill its obligation. Haunted by visions of the hangman's noose or enslavement, Librán languished in his shackles. Then, at the very last minute, a wealthy relative stepped forward with full payment for the victim's kin. By such an act, the kinsman had bought Librán's life; he now quite literally owned

THE SEASONAL ROUND

Evoking the bellowing of mythic bulls, the blare of bronze or wooden horns heralded the great festivals of Celtic Ireland. Celebrated on November 1, Samhain marked the return of herds from summer pasture, the onset of winter, and the start of a new year. It was a time of weddings, and many births followed the harvest festival, Lughnasadh, nine months later. Completing the Celtic sacred cycle were Imbolc on February 1 and Beltane on May 1. These festivals signaled the arrivals of spring and summer.

Librán, who had to wear a special slave belt in token of his new status.

But within a matter of days he broke his oath and fled the home of the kinsman who had ransomed him. Librán had determined to do penance for his sins, and he crossed the sea to seek sanctuary on the Scottish island of Iona in the monastery of Columba. He was now a fugitive from justice—an absconder, in Irish legal terms—and not even a priest of Columba's eminence could legally give him asylum. Still, the monk wanted to help him. First he tested the strength of Librán's penitence by describing the burdens of monastic life. Librán was unfazed. "I am ready for anything you choose to demand of me," he declared, "however harsh, however degrading." Then Columba ordered him to spend seven years in penance at Mag Luinge, a monastery and a "house for penitents" on the island of Tiree, northwest of Iona.

Librán faithfully carried out these orders, returning to Iona only when the seven years were over. He then repeated to Columba his concern about his broken oath of servitude to the kinsman who had saved him. Columba instructed Librán to go home to Ireland and handed him an elegant sword decorated with carved ivory. He was to offer the weapon to his former master as a gift in exchange for his liberty.

After receiving Columba's blessing, Librán returned to his native district. When he presented the sword to his kinsman, the latter was ready to accept it as the price of Librán's freedom; the kinsman's wife was not. "How can we accept this precious gift which Columba has sent?" she asked. "Let this dutiful servant be delivered to the saint without payment. For the holy man's blessing will bring us more benefit than this gift which is offered." Heeding this shrewd advice, her husband reached out and untied the captive's belt that his former slave had continued to wear all those years. With that gesture, he released Librán from his sworn obligation and from servitude.

A major hurdle had been overcome, but Librán still faced another weighty legal obligation. In his absence from home he had become what was termed an "undutiful son." According to Irish law, it was the responsibility of every son to care for his parents in their declining years. The law regarded parental care so highly, in fact, that a man without sons was allowed to adopt someone from outside his kinship group to look after him and his wife in their old age. So when Librán's brothers reminded him that he had neglected his duty, Librán was not surprised, and without complaint he agreed to help take care of his mother and father.

Impressed that Librán had been "working for the salvation of his soul," however, one of his younger brothers volunteered to take on Librán's share of the responsibilities. This generous gesture liberated Librán from the last remaining legal tie that bound him to Connacht and his old way of life. Bidding his family farewell, he made his way to the northern port of Derry and headed back to Iona.

Reaching the monastery, Librán returned the valuable sword to Columba. The monk then administered the monastic vow to Librán and sent him again to Mag Luinge, where he had served out his time of penance. There, for many years, he lived the simple life of the monk. He was known as "Librán of the reed-bed" because his special task was to gather reeds that were presumably used to thatch roofs in the monastery.

"When he was a very old man," wrote Librán's chronicler, Adomnán, "he was sent to Ireland on some business of the community." He was hospitably received in the guesthouse at the monastery of Durrow in central Ireland, but soon fell ill. A week later, Librán died. According to Adomnán, "There he was buried among the elect monks of Saint Columba, where he will rise again to eternal life."

An excerpt from an eighth-century law text considers the rights of women, which in early Ireland were defined by their relationships to men. Recorded in smaller script between the lines are explanatory notes and comments made by jurists several centuries later.

As the son of a small farmer in early Ireland, Librán had grown up in a world that offered him few opportunities to escape his assigned lot in life. The choices for Irishwomen were fewer still. Under Irish law, for example, a woman was considered legally incompetent, with scarcely more legal standing than a slave or a child. In practically all legal matters she needed a man to act for her, and she could not give testimony or enter into a contract without the consent of a male guardian. The identity of these guardians changed over the course of a female's life. In the words of an early law text, "Her father has charge over her when she is a girl, her husband when she is a wife, her sons when she is a [widowed] woman with children."

The inferior legal and social status of females was nowhere more evident than in that key measure of individual material value, the honor price. At age 14, for instance, a boy merited full honor price, while a girl was worth only half of her father's honor price; when she married it became half of her husband's. Even a crime against a woman was normally regarded as a crime against her guardian—to be compensated by the offender's payment of *his* honor price, not hers.

Society's expectations of women were summed up in the familiar phrase "three drops of a wedded woman," drops of blood, sweat, and tears. In other words, a young woman should be a virgin at marriage, should work hard to support her husband and children, and should be willing to suffer on her family's behalf. She was also required to have "a steady tongue, a steady virtue, and a steady housewifery." This view of woman as industrious, virtuous, and submissive contrasted sharply with the images of Irish female warriors and fertility goddesses—like the legendary Maeve, the spear-toting, boisterous, and lustful queen of Connacht—who strode defiantly through the Celtic sagas.

To better understand the life of an Irish wife of the seventh century, let us imagine a young woman we will call Clíodna. Imagine, too, that Clíodna is on the verge of marriage, a state that both she and her parents would have eagerly sought. To be sure, marriage would perpetuate many aspects of her legal inferiority: Her husband would be her superior legally and socially. And she would be taken from the security of her own extended family and plunged into the unfamiliarity of her husband's fine. But marriage would also probably bring her a measure of independence, gain her the ownership of property, and secure her place in the Irish economy. Most of all, however, it would fulfill her destiny as an Irishwoman by providing heirs for her husband's lineage.

By custom, Clíodna's family would begin the process that propelled her into marriage. They might take into consideration her own feelings for a particular man, but marriage was considered an economic partnership rather than an affair of the heart. They would select the groom, choosing from a list of candidates they considered of suitable social rank. If her father was a *bóaire*—literally, a "strong farmer," with about twice as much land as Librán's father—he would have wanted his daughter to marry the son of another bóaire. And though the church and Irish law frowned upon incest, her father may even have picked for her a groom from his own extended family, a distant cousin, perhaps, in order to keep everything within the fine.

After selecting a suitable prospect, Clíodna's family would also decide the type of marriage. Of the nine different forms of sexual union recognized by Irish law, her family would hope for the so-called union of joint property because it was the most prestigious and generally the most advantageous to the bride. In this form of union, both partners contributed an equal amount of marriage property—the *tinól*—for establishing the household. The tinól was provided by the two families and usually included butter churns and implements for traditional feminine tasks, as well as the customary male farming tools. This type of marriage would make Clíodna, in the words of the law, "a woman of equal lordship." If necessary, she legally could manage the farm on her own, and her husband could not make contracts or other major business transactions without her permission.

The details of the marriage contract would be hammered out in negotiations with the family of

Although it has been suggested that stone carvings of female figures known as sheela-na-gigs were associated with a pre-Christian Irish fertility cult, their exact function is unknown.

the groom. Then the groom would present to the parents and the bride a prenuptial gift, which in Clíodna's case probably would have been two cows. This presentation occurred in front of witnesses and served as proof that a marriage contract had indeed been agreed upon. After the pooling of goods for the tinól, a public wedding ceremony accompanied by an appropriate feast usually completed the nuptials.

It would not have been surprising if Clíodna had later been forced to share her new husband with other wives, however. Despite church opposition, multiple marriage could legally be practiced by men—but not by women—and frequently was. Furthermore, male offspring from all marriages enjoyed equal inheritance rights in the husband's fine.

But as the first woman to wed her husband, Clíodna would be regarded as his chief wife, and any other spouses would be considered concubines, or secondary wives. And a secondary wife was just that: She was usually assigned only half the status and entitlements of the chief wife. In fact, the chief wife could physically assault and injure her with impunity, while her own right to retaliate was limited to scratching, pulling hair, or speaking abusively. Perhaps understandably, the husband had to maintain separate residences for his wives. His principal home, though, was

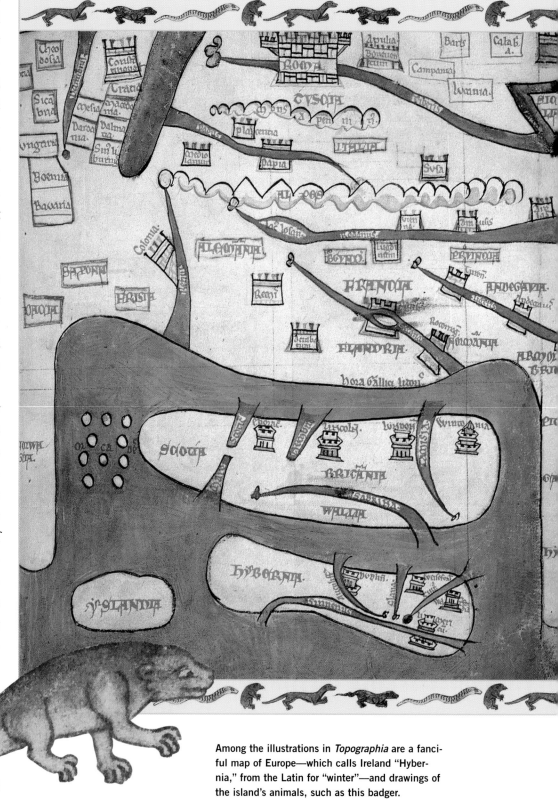

Among the illustrations in *Topographia* are a fanciful map of Europe—which calls Ireland "Hybernia," from the Latin for "winter"—and drawings of the island's animals, such as this badger.

a traveler's diary, 1189

They were "a filthy people wallowing in vice," concluded one foreigner about the Irish he met while traveling in their country in the late 12th century. The foreigner was Giraldus Cambrensis, better known as Gerald of Wales, a priest and historian dispatched by his king, Henry II of England, to gather information about the island and its inhabitants. The results of his work were published in 1189 as *Topographia Hiberniae*, or *The History and Topography of Ireland.*

Just how much Gerald saw of Ireland is not known. He may have visited a number of ports, from Cork and Waterford in the south to Arklow, Wicklow, and Dublin in the east. He also seems to have traveled to Meath and Kildare, and probably made it as far west as the Shannon. But his knowledge of the interior is sketchy at best, and he may well have journeyed from place to place by ship rather than by more-hazardous land routes.

Whatever the extent of Gerald's trav-

In the "Wonders and Miracles" section of *Topographia*, Gerald of Wales relates the tale of Saint Kevin, shown at left holding a blackbird. According to legend, when the bird landed on his outstretched hand and laid her eggs there, the saint patiently held his hand in the same position until her offspring were hatched.

77

els, *Topographia Hiberniae* is still the source of most of what we know about life in early Ireland—its landscape, climate, and wildlife, as well as the people who lived there. It is clear, however, that Gerald often skewed his descriptions in favor of England and never allowed the truth to get in the way of a good story.

Gerald had an eye for the freakish and the fantastic, sights that were "contrary to nature's course" and "worthy of wonder." He wrote of "a woman with a beard and a mane on her back," for instance, and "a man that was half an ox and an ox that was half a man." Among the wondrous animals he described were "a wolf that talked with a priest," "a fish with three gold teeth," and "a cow that was partly a stag." To Gerald even the landscape was filled with the bizarre. He mentioned

Although he found few reasons to praise the Irish, the Welshman did note the "incomparable skill of the people in musical instruments."

Gerald expressed alarm at the common Irish custom of carrying "an axe in their hand as if it were a staff" to "inflict a mortal blow."

78

In his book Gerald marveled at two Irish sailors from a remote area who had "heard nothing of Christ."

"two islands in one of which no one dies" and "a whirlpool of the sea that swallows ships."

Perhaps anticipating a skeptical reception, Gerald stood by his *Topographia.* "I protest solemnly," he wrote, "that I have put down nothing in this book the truth of which I have not found out either by the testimony of my own eyes, or that of reliable men." The illustrations on this and the previous pages were executed by Gerald himself. They portray some of the wonders he encountered in Celtic Ireland and what life there, at least to him, was really like.

with his chief wife; bringing a secondary wife there was cause for divorce.

This was just one of a surprising number of different reasons for divorce recognized by Irish law. Most, as might be expected in a patriarchal society, were weighted in favor of the male. A husband could divorce his wife, for example, if she was unfaithful, procured an abortion, smothered her child, practiced thievery, or otherwise brought dishonor on her husband's name. On the other hand, she could divorce him if he had tricked her into marriage by sorcery, struck her with enough force to leave a permanent scar, or grew too fat. She could also seek a divorce if he talked too much in public about the intimate details of their marriage—"because it is not right for a man who tells of bed to be under blankets." If a wife left her husband without a reason deemed just by the law, however, she would be stripped of all status and rights in Irish society.

As the wife of a bóaire, Clíodna would live in a domain largely defined by the ring-fort. In the farmyard within its rampart, she helped milk the cows, churned butter and made cheese, and fattened the pigs on whey and table scraps. Inside her round wattle-and-daub home —a structure larger than those of the poorer Libráns of the world but still probably less than 600 square feet in area—she kept house in a primitive fashion. The

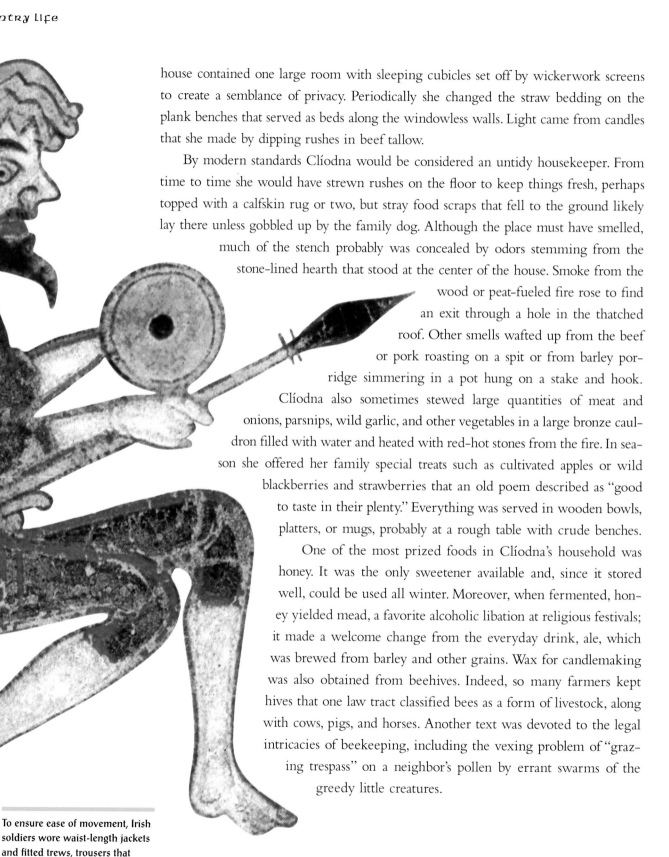

To ensure ease of movement, Irish soldiers wore waist-length jackets and fitted trews, trousers that reached below the knee.

house contained one large room with sleeping cubicles set off by wickerwork screens to create a semblance of privacy. Periodically she changed the straw bedding on the plank benches that served as beds along the windowless walls. Light came from candles that she made by dipping rushes in beef tallow.

By modern standards Clíodna would be considered an untidy housekeeper. From time to time she would have strewn rushes on the floor to keep things fresh, perhaps topped with a calfskin rug or two, but stray food scraps that fell to the ground likely lay there unless gobbled up by the family dog. Although the place must have smelled, much of the stench probably was concealed by odors stemming from the stone-lined hearth that stood at the center of the house. Smoke from the wood or peat-fueled fire rose to find an exit through a hole in the thatched roof. Other smells wafted up from the beef or pork roasting on a spit or from barley porridge simmering in a pot hung on a stake and hook. Clíodna also sometimes stewed large quantities of meat and onions, parsnips, wild garlic, and other vegetables in a large bronze cauldron filled with water and heated with red-hot stones from the fire. In season she offered her family special treats such as cultivated apples or wild blackberries and strawberries that an old poem described as "good to taste in their plenty." Everything was served in wooden bowls, platters, or mugs, probably at a rough table with crude benches.

One of the most prized foods in Clíodna's household was honey. It was the only sweetener available and, since it stored well, could be used all winter. Moreover, when fermented, honey yielded mead, a favorite alcoholic libation at religious festivals; it made a welcome change from the everyday drink, ale, which was brewed from barley and other grains. Wax for candlemaking was also obtained from beehives. Indeed, so many farmers kept hives that one law tract classified bees as a form of livestock, along with cows, pigs, and horses. Another text was devoted to the legal intricacies of beekeeping, including the vexing problem of "grazing trespass" on a neighbor's pollen by errant swarms of the greedy little creatures.

By Clíodna's day, one of the most dreaded household tasks—the drudgery of grinding grain into flour—had been transformed for some into a social pleasure. Until the introduction of water-powered mills in the early seventh century, all grain had been ground by hand between two stones. The change to water power was so revolutionary that a charming legend to explain it took root: King Cormac of Tara, it was said, had introduced the first water mill out of pity for his pregnant mistress, a slave girl, who had grown weary of hand grinding. As for Clíodna, her husband probably owned a share in a mill together with neighbors and kinsmen. Such mills soon became a focus of community for women who lived on isolated farmsteads. While waiting for the flour to emerge from the mill's chute, they could take the opportunity to talk and form social ties.

Clíodna and other women would also get together and socialize while performing one of the most prized of female occupations—the production of wool and linen cloth, a laborious and time-consuming process made less onerous by having company. The fleece of the small brown Irish sheep had to be shorn, teased and combed, spun by hand into yarn, dyed, and then woven into cloth. The woolen cloth next had to be scoured to remove its natural lanolin and fulled—steeped in cold water with vegetable ash or stale human urine and trampled—to shrink it in order to achieve greater density and a softer finish. Linen was even more demanding. The flax plant had to be harvested, combed to remove the seeds, and then soaked in water, beaten, and scraped to free the fibers from the stalk. The fibers were combed and separated before being spun into thread, dyed, and woven into linen cloth. After all this, of course, Clíodna and her companions had to fashion the fabrics into cloaks, tunics, and other garments. Some of these items would be for use by their own families; the rest were traded.

The only female function valued more than the production of cloth was reproduction itself. Childbearing—especially of legitimate male heirs—was of such overriding importance that a woman's infertility was legal cause for divorce. Clíodna may well have been expected to bear children over a period of nearly two decades, giving birth perhaps five or six times. If she was fortunate, half of her offspring might survive the diseases endemic to infancy and childhood. Ironically, however, she would probably not have the experience of raising these survivors to adulthood. Among families of her class, and especially among the nobility, it was customary to farm out sons and daughters at around the age of seven. At that time they were handed over to families who would complete the process of child rearing by training them, a practice called fosterage.

In Clíodna's case, the foster parents might well be from her own extended family. A brother, for instance, might take in one of her children as a matter of affection as well as obligation. But parents could also pay a suitable family to foster their offspring. Irish law prescribed a fee scale ranging from one and a half cows for the son of a small farmer to 15 cows for a king's son; foster fees for girls ran

Made from a single piece of leather and sewn into shape with gut, this shoe may have warmed the foot of a wealthy Irishman.

slightly higher, perhaps because they were thought to require more care. Boys typically remained in fosterage until they were around 17 years old, girls until about 14. During that period, the foster parents maintained and trained the child according to the status of the biological father or the youngster's assigned station in Irish society. The son of a small farmer, for example, learned to herd livestock and cultivate the land; the daughter was taught to milk, keep house, and cook. The son of a blacksmith would be placed in fosterage with a blacksmith; children intended for the church, with clerics.

Although the law texts set out the legal aspects of the institution—it required a formal contract bound by sureties—fosterage typically developed strong personal ties of affection and intimacy. One measure of this closeness was the fact that it was the foster mother and father, not the biological ones, who were called Mommy and Daddy. The lifelong bonds that evolved between foster brothers often proved to be tighter than those between blood brothers. It was almost certainly the need for a network of relationships extending beyond the family that explained the prevalence of fosterage among the nobility, who were always on the lookout for new political alliances.

Such, then, was the lot of an Irish wife of the seventh century, to make food and clothing and raise someone else's children. And although she probably fared better than her counterparts on the Continent, she must always have been aware of her legal inferiority to her husband and of the role society demanded of her. In early Ireland there were few ways women could avoid this kind of an existence. But one alternative was offered by the church: taking up the veil and becoming a nun. One who chose this way of life during the mid-eighth century was a young woman known as Cummen.

Like the girls with whom she had grown up, Cummen had always known she had no choice but to marry. But she knew, too, that the law did provide a choice about *whom* she could marry. As one text declared, "At a proper age a girl should be betrothed to God or to a man." In other words, she could reject all secular suitors and become a so-called bride of Christ.

Why Cummen became a nun is left unrecorded. The circumstances behind her decision were presumably far less dramatic than the desperate yearning for ecclesiastical penance that had driven the remorseful Librán less than two centuries earlier.

Cummen may have become intrigued with the possibility during a visit to a nearby monastery, church, or saint's shrine. She might have gone there for celebration of a Christian ritual or to seek counsel from a high-ranking monk or nun. In the latter instance, she may have been advised that marrying Christ would give her economic support, physical protection, and many of the other benefits of secular marriage. Almost certainly she would have been told that a spiritual union would bring her a gift not guaranteed to mere laywomen: salvation.

Nevertheless, even as she pursued the nun's lot of self-denial, prayer, and contemplation, Cummen was still heavily dependent on males. Of the many convents available to Irishwomen, most were situated next to or near monasteries. In fact, she and the other nuns would have served as housekeepers for the monks, cooking their meals and taking care of their laundry. Such close everyday contacts with the opposite sex did not extend to worship, however. In churches, monks and nuns commonly practiced segregated prayer with a wall dividing them. And in the eighth century it was decreed that no woman, even a bride of Christ, could enter a monastery's holiest place, its sanctuary.

All the same, Cummen did possess legal rights seldom available to her secular sisters. For example, she could provide legal evidence, buy property, manage a farm, and generally transact business on her own. These prerogatives stemmed from her status as a nun and as a woman of wealth. The source of her wealth, while not recorded, most likely lay in gifts from her immediate family and other kinsmen. A woman could legally inherit land that her mother had gained by gift or by her own labor, but only if she had no brothers. A father might also defy law and tradition by presenting parcels of property to his daughters to compensate for the fact that only his sons could inherit land after his death. These gifts usually caused turmoil in the larger kinship group, however, which did not want to see the land pass out of its control; even when a daughter inherited her father's land because she had no brothers, control of it reverted to the group upon her death. But women who took the veil had another option: They might sell such land or give it as a grant to the church.

Cummen used the wealth she brought with her to purchase a farming estate. In partnership with a person known as Brethán but otherwise not identified, she bought in Connacht a place called Óchter Achid—"with its (whole) estates, in wood, plain, and meadow, with its enclosure and its herb-garden." Cummen probably intended to start a small convent at Óchter Achid, where she could live with a few like-minded others, perhaps relatives who had also taken the veil. Such religious communities had

PRACTICE MAKES PERFECT

Before creating actual metalwork, Irish artisans sometimes practiced their decorative art on trial pieces like this polished bone from the eighth or early ninth century. Its intricate interlacing and knotwork designs are frequently employed in Celtic art and were carved either by a craftsman perfecting his technique or by an apprentice in training.

Three modestly garbed females adorning a bronze house shrine may be nuns, a respectable calling for Irishwomen and one endorsed by Saint Patrick. Some women who eschewed marriage and the secular world, like Saint Brigit, enjoyed considerable status as abbesses of prominent monasteries.

their own farms with livestock and cultivated fields, relying on hired lay clients to perform much of the farm work.

Whatever her intentions for the estate, Cummen wanted to buy out her partner Brethán and become the sole owner. To purchase the other half, she planned to use her tinól, or marriage property. Since Irish law validated spiritual union, the fact that Cummen had married Christ instead of an Irishman did not prevent her from receiving this property. Cummen's tinól is itemized in the *Book of Armagh,* a collection of biographical writings compiled by scholars at the great church located there. The tinól included three ounces of silver, a necklace worth three ounces of silver, a circlet of gold, and a number of pigs and sheep. It was a generous sum indeed, the equivalent of somewhere between five and 10 cows.

Though the tinól customarily was given just before marriage, there may have been a delay in presenting the property to Cummen. Perhaps some members of her family had opposed her choice of a religious union over a secular one. But even after the property was turned over, it evidently was not enough for the purchase of Brethán's half of the estate. To raise the remainder of the necessary capital, Cummen relied on the special skills expected of all Irishwomen: the production and refinement of cloth. With wool presumably shorn from sheep on her estate and dye from local plants, she spun, wove, and decorated a handsome mantle to adorn the shoulders of a man who could afford it.

To sell her mantle, Cummen may have attended one of the regional market fairs. These gatherings often took place at large monasteries and attracted jewelers and other craftsmen eager to trade their wares. The commercial transactions were attended by lively entertainments: Horses were raced, men engaged in athletic contests, and jugglers and buffoons performed. The record indicates that Cummen succeeded in trading her mantle to a nobleman for a valuable brown horse. She then sold the horse to a second man for an amount of silver bullion.

This silver, together with her tinól, enabled Cummen to complete the purchase of the other half of Óchter Achid. The inclusion of her transaction in the *Book of Armagh* suggests she may have intended to will the estate to that church. Though Armagh was in the northeast of the country, it was the hub of a wide network of smaller congregations and religious communities. By presenting Óchter Achid as a gift to Armagh, Cummen would have continued to serve long after death as a faithful, productive, and revered bride of the church.

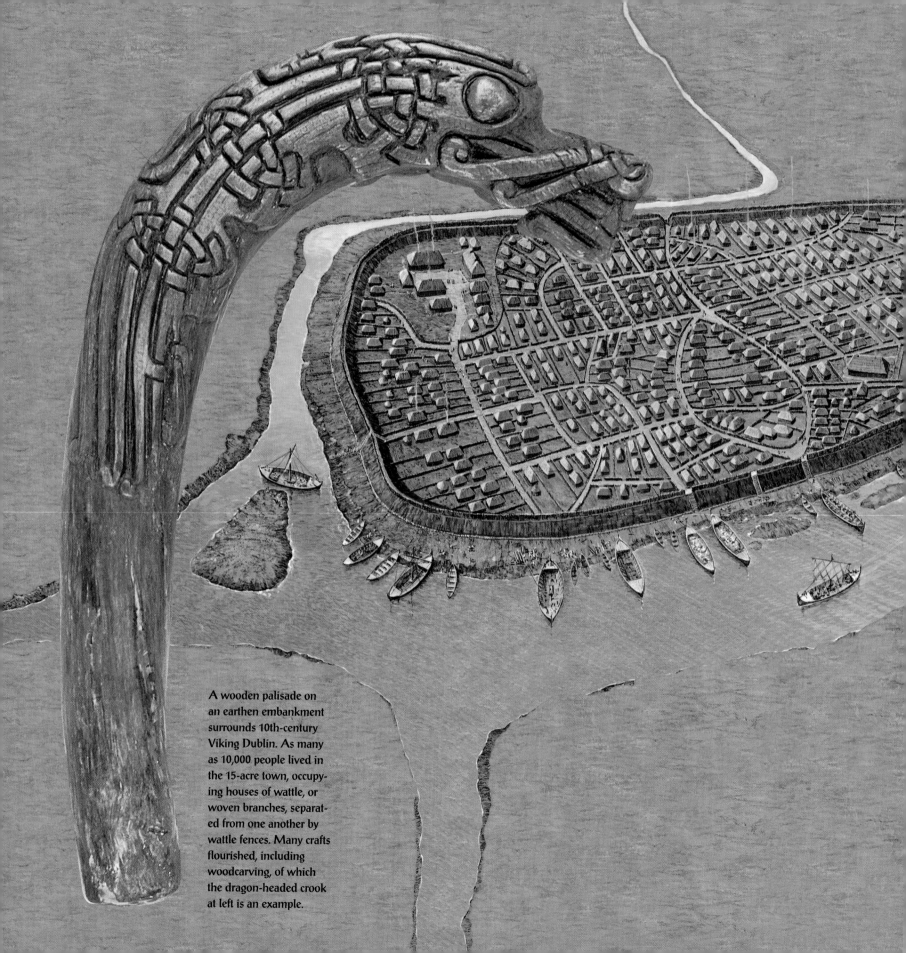

A wooden palisade on an earthen embankment surrounds 10th-century Viking Dublin. As many as 10,000 people lived in the 15-acre town, occupying houses of wattle, or woven branches, separated from one another by wattle fences. Many crafts flourished, including woodcarving, of which the dragon-headed crook at left is an example.

DUBLIN: a VIKING CITY

The Vikings may have been vagabonds, descending on Ireland in "immense floods and countless sea-vomitings of ships and boats" and sowing destruction wherever they came ashore, but they did something unusual for raiders—some eventually settled down and made Ireland their home. Indeed, if it had not been for the Vikings, there might not be a Dublin, Waterford, Cork, Limerick, or Wexford—all cities in Ireland founded by them.

Chief of these cities, Viking Dublin, began as a winter camp in 841, a site chosen for its location at an important ford across the River Liffey where the main roads north, south, and southwest came together. Its name commemorates its origins: There was a small settlement there before the Norse arrived. The Irish called it Dubh Linn, for the so-called black pool at the confluence of the Rivers Poddle and Liffey that would serve the Vikings as a harbor. From this base the newcomers sailed out on raiding and trading expeditions until a coalition of Irish kings temporarily drove them from Ireland in 902.

After spending some years abroad, mainly in England and Scotland, the Vikings returned to the area in 917 and established a new and prosperous settlement. The Irish kings, tantalized by Dublin's wealth, exerted increasing pressure on the community. The Vikings eventually yielded, paying tribute to the Irish and even putting their fleet and themselves at the service of one or another of the kings during Ireland's internecine struggles. By the time the Scandinavians were fully assimilated, Dublin had become a great international port.

This map shows the first true towns of Ireland, founded by the Vikings. With their excellent access to the sea, these towns became part of the Viking trading network that extended from Scandinavia east into Russia, west to Iceland, around the Irish Sea, and south into the Mediterranean.

LARNE

ANNAGASSAN
NAVAN
EYREPHORT
DUBLIN

CASTLEDERMOT
WICKLOW
KILLALOE
THURLES
LIMERICK
CASHEL
ARKLOW

WEXFORD
WATERFORD

CORK

a Bustling marketplace

Viking Dublin grew rich through trade, especially through its commerce with population centers in England. But the city dealt in more than durable goods: One of the most frequently traded commodities was slaves. The unfortunates were often captured during raids conducted by Irish lords against their rivals, sold in Dublin to traders, and then shipped to England, Iceland, and Scandinavia for resale. By the 11th century, Dublin had emerged as one of the major slave markets in western Europe.

As the Vikings prospered, goods and raw materials from all over flowed into the market town—amber from the Baltic, silk from the East, and silver and silver coins from Germany and western and central Asia. According to an old Irish account, the streets of Dublin were "filled with the wealth of barbarians."

It was silver, however, that counted most. Not only was it regarded as a measure of a man's wealth, but it could also be used in daily commerce. Coins, necklaces, and armbands were often cut into pieces—hack silver, as it was called—to buy goods according to the fragments' weight and worth.

To serve the everyday needs of the population and supply the export market, leatherworkers made shoes and sword scabbards; woodworkers turned out bowls, platters, and other vessels on their lathes. One group of craftsmen produced combs and ornaments from bone and antler. Others built boats of all kinds, including the vessels that Irish kings used to control the interior rivers.

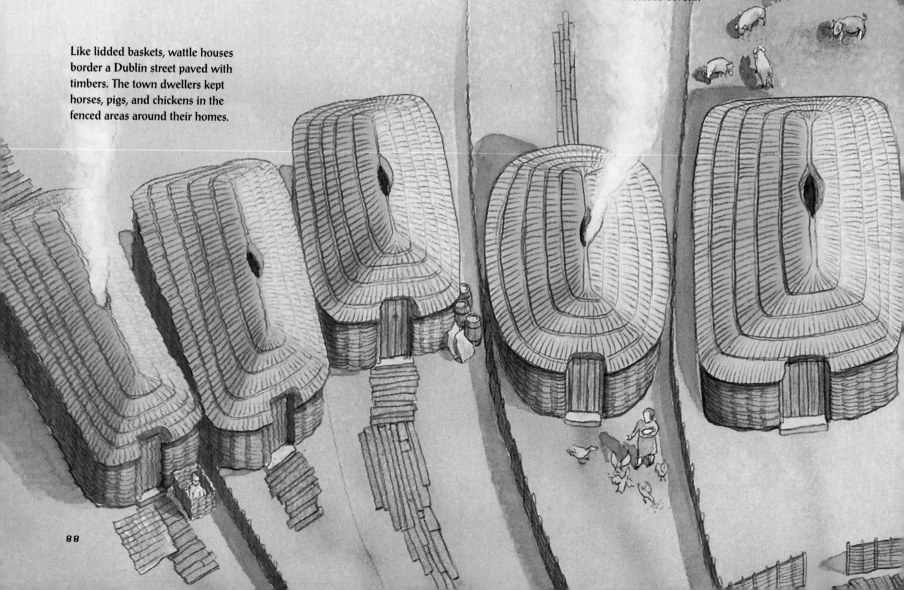

Like lidded baskets, wattle houses border a Dublin street paved with timbers. The town dwellers kept horses, pigs, and chickens in the fenced areas around their homes.

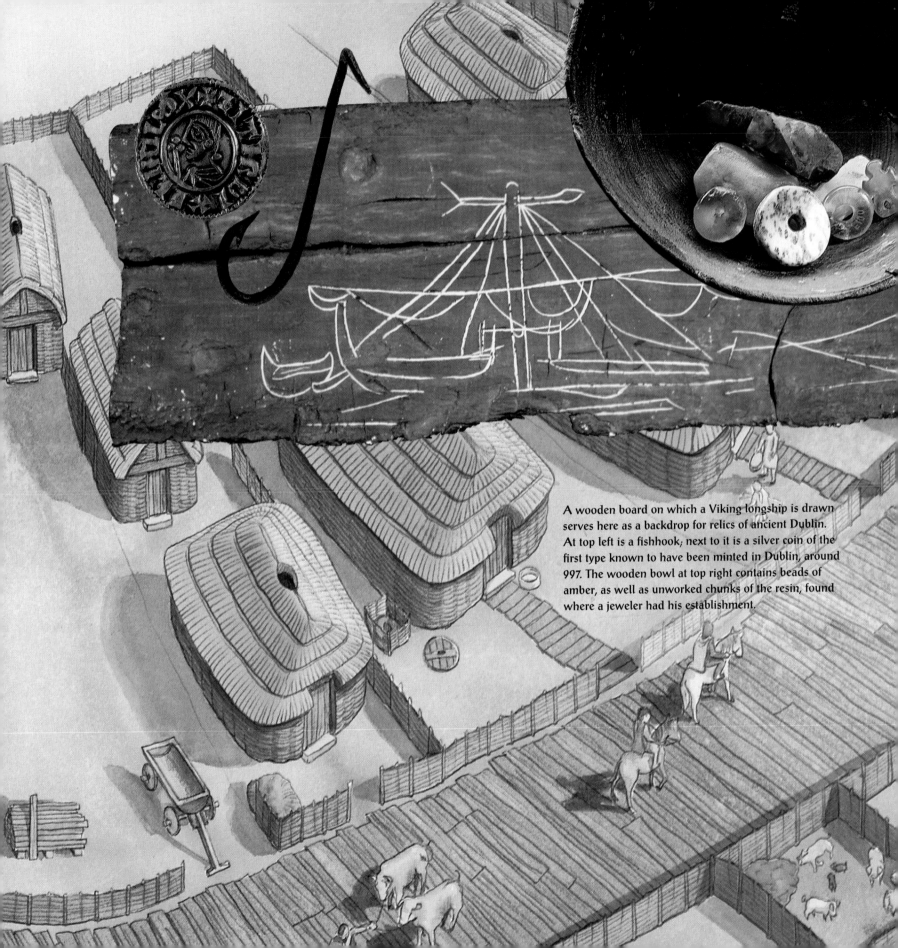

A wooden board on which a Viking longship is drawn serves here as a backdrop for relics of ancient Dublin. At top left is a fishhook; next to it is a silver coin of the first type known to have been minted in Dublin, around 997. The wooden bowl at top right contains beads of amber, as well as unworked chunks of the resin, found where a jeweler had his establishment.

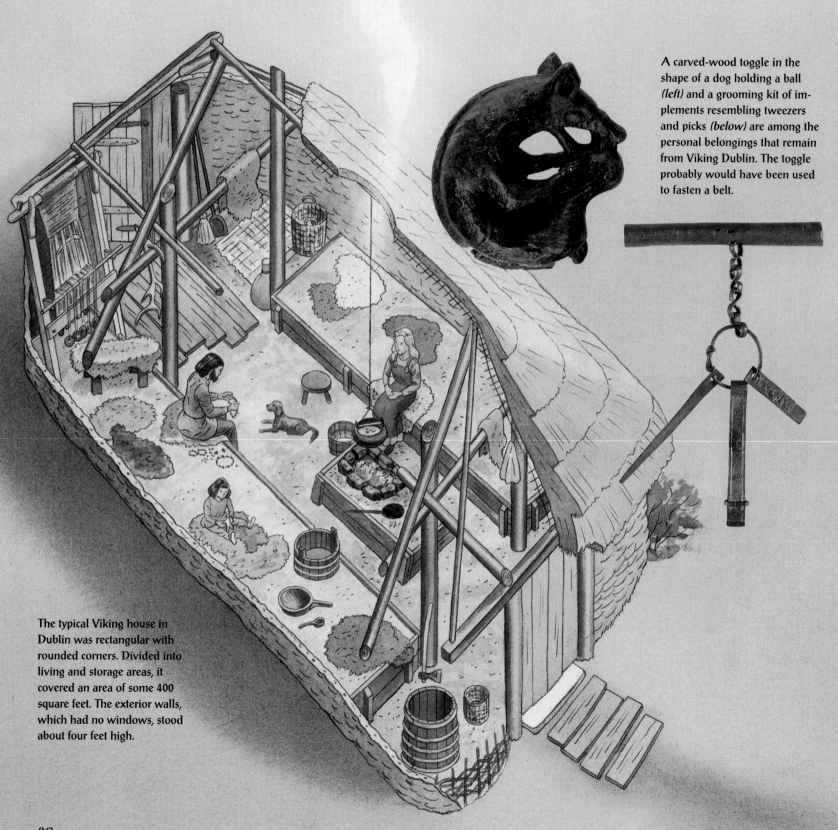

A carved-wood toggle in the shape of a dog holding a ball *(left)* and a grooming kit of implements resembling tweezers and picks *(below)* are among the personal belongings that remain from Viking Dublin. The toggle probably would have been used to fasten a belt.

The typical Viking house in Dublin was rectangular with rounded corners. Divided into living and storage areas, it covered an area of some 400 square feet. The exterior walls, which had no windows, stood about four feet high.

hearth and home

No matter what an individual's wealth or station in old Dublin may have been, life in a wattle house could not have been very comfortable. For one thing, there was the cold and damp of the climate to contend with; for another, there was the constant threat of flooding by the River Liffey.

It comes as no surprise, then, that the Vikings' houses lasted no more than 10 to 20 years, their posts rotting at the bases and forcing evacuation before the thatch roofs they supported, underlaid with a layer of sod, gave way. But a new house must have been a lovely thing, smelling sweetly of the twined branches that formed the layers of its walls and of the moss and ferns sometimes stuffed between them for insulation. All too soon, however, the house would be permeated by the smoke from the hearth in the middle of the room and by the soot that turned the wattle black.

A wide aisle occupied the center of the dwelling, with benches on either side. The floor was of trampled earth, sometimes covered with wattle mats. The interior walls may have been hung with textile screens or woven basketry for insulation. A corner was sometimes set aside for domestic chores or craft production. Barrels, churns, and workbenches have been found in these areas.

To protect themselves against the damp chill, the people wore thick clothing of coarse wool, using silk neckerchiefs to keep their skin from being chafed, and slept on the benches that lined the walls and were heaped with brush and straw and covered with animal hides and fleeces. In spite of the drabness of their surroundings, or perhaps because of it, the Vikings were known for their brightly colored clothing and for their fine adornments—silver brooches, beaded necklaces, gold rings, and carved-bone hairpins.

Among Dubliners' prized possessions were combs for tending the long hair favored by both sexes. The one below is made of carved and decorated bone and comes with a matching case.

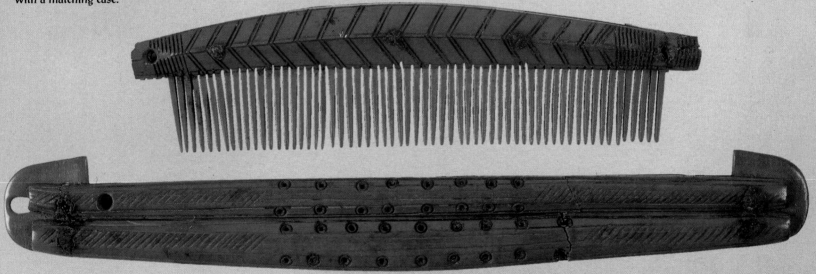

a high king for Ireland

The Munster warriors of King Brian Boru attack their Irish and Norse enemies in this 19th-century painting of the Battle of Clontarf, fought outside Dublin in 1014. Brian's men reportedly wore "crested golden helmets" but little body armor, and carried shields, swords, axes, spears, and darts. They defeated a rival army "encased from head to foot" in metal.

Even at the age of 58, the king of Munster had lost none of his swagger. Admittedly, his long hair was now streaked with silver and his brow perennially furrowed with care. But Brian Boru was as wary and as dangerous as ever. And though the years had added bulk to his frame, enough muscle still rippled beneath his linen tunic to recall younger days and distant battles, when the man who would be high king had snatched up the standard of his fallen brother and had made himself the master of the hillocked chessboard that was 10th-century Ireland. One by one, in the waning decades of that century, lesser kings had become his pawns, towers and fortifications his spoils, bishops the beneficiaries of his largess, and at least one other king's wife his own.

Now, as the last days of the first millennium drained from the year 999, Brian found himself again on the attack, this time on the outskirts of Viking Dublin. Around him his troops shuffled restlessly in place, some worrying the handles of spears, others, their jaws set, testing the hilts of swords. Yet for all their resolve, few of these men were professional soldiers, and those few likely to have been mercenaries. The rest were recruits—freemen responding to their king's call for what the Irish called a "hosting."

While he readied his men for battle, Brian might well have walked among them, lending a word of encouragement here, snapping an order there, bucking up one of the many youths for whom the day's blood would prove a test of manhood. As for himself, he was itching to show those upstarts who dared oppose his kingship that he was the lord to whom they owed loyalty. Here at Glen Máma, he vowed, here in the green-carpeted "Glen of the Gap" just south of Dublin, he would bring to their knees both Dublin's Viking king, Sitriuc, who for 10 years had been Brian's own step-son, and Sitriuc's uncle, Máel Mórda, king of Leinster.

With dawn ribboning a cloud-scudded sky, the two armies closed in on each other. "And there was fought between them," recounts a later chronicle in a flurry of adjectives, "a battle, bloody, furious, red, valiant, heroic, manly; rough, cruel, heartless." Sword rang upon sword in the damp December air, Munster axes cleft Leinster bone, spears sank with a thud into wooden shields, while all around the grunts of those still struggling formed a macabre counterpoint to the groans of those then dying.

Where thousands had fought, 4,000 and more of the enemy were dead by day's end. Victory won, Brian Boru and his men marched into Dublin and burned the city. "Many women also, and boys, and girls, were brought to bondage and ruin by them," as one Irish saga tells the tale. Máel Mórda was flushed ignominiously from hiding in a yew tree and Sitriuc was driven out on the point of a sword.

Refused refuge everywhere else in Ireland, Sitriuc soon enough came slinking back to Dublin and there formally submitted to his former stepfather. In time-honored fash-ion, the chastened Norseman pledged his loyalty to Brian and guaranteed his submis-sion by turning over a handful of his own subjects as hostages. "He is not a king who does not have hostages in fetters," reads one Irish legal text, advice that Brian Boru, proud sovereign that he'd long been, would surely have heeded. The most potent hostages for the Munster king would have been members of Sitriuc's own family, since the nearer and dearer the collat-eral, went the thinking,

This iron collar may have encircled the neck of a hostage given as a guarantee that tribute pledged would be paid. Hostages were a sign of prestige for Irish kings.

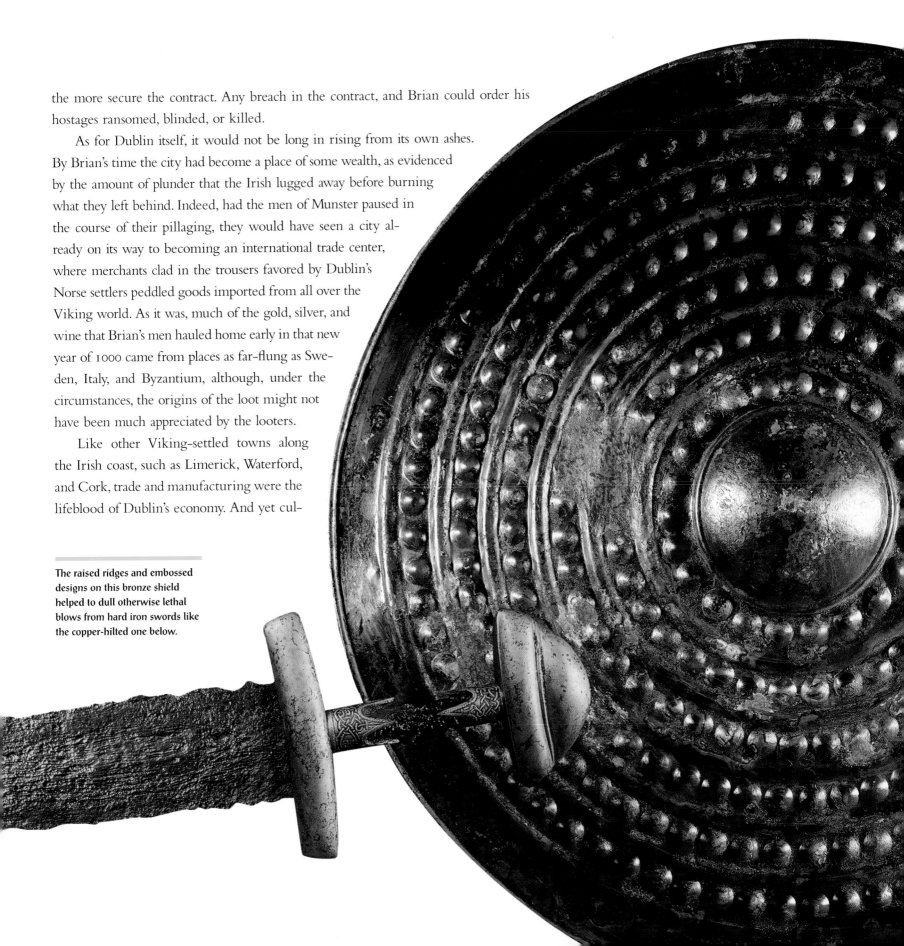

the more secure the contract. Any breach in the contract, and Brian could order his hostages ransomed, blinded, or killed.

As for Dublin itself, it would not be long in rising from its own ashes. By Brian's time the city had become a place of some wealth, as evidenced by the amount of plunder that the Irish lugged away before burning what they left behind. Indeed, had the men of Munster paused in the course of their pillaging, they would have seen a city already on its way to becoming an international trade center, where merchants clad in the trousers favored by Dublin's Norse settlers peddled goods imported from all over the Viking world. As it was, much of the gold, silver, and wine that Brian's men hauled home early in that new year of 1000 came from places as far-flung as Sweden, Italy, and Byzantium, although, under the circumstances, the origins of the loot might not have been much appreciated by the looters.

Like other Viking-settled towns along the Irish coast, such as Limerick, Waterford, and Cork, trade and manufacturing were the lifeblood of Dublin's economy. And yet cul-

The raised ridges and embossed designs on this bronze shield helped to dull otherwise lethal blows from hard iron swords like the copper-hilted one below.

turally the Viking influence was on the wane as the descendants of the original settlers gradually melted into Irish society. Of course, whether Dubliners were of Irish or Viking stock or what they did for a living would have mattered less to Brian Boru than the simple fact that they had dared challenge his own authority as overking. Yet, even as Brian Boru savored his triumph over the combined forces of Máel Mórda and Sitriuc at Glen Máma, he was already eyeing a loftier prize—that of *ard-rí,* the high kingship, and with it unchallenged control of all Ireland.

Brian's rise to power had begun some 20 years earlier in 976 with the slaying of his older brother by a rival king. Succeeding his brother as ruler of Dál Cais, a kingdom in the southwest of Ireland, Brian immediately set out to avenge the death, leaving his enemies' blood splashed the length and breadth of Munster.

Munster was itself one of the five historical provinces that were known collectively as the Fifths, the others being Leinster, Ulster, Connacht, and Meath. These were in turn composed of some 150 *túatha,* or kingdoms, which, like the *túath* of Dál Cais, had originally been tribal in nature and structure. Up to the eighth century, each of these túatha had had its own king, in accordance with an ancient legal maxim: "That is no túath that has no king."

In this earlier period, the king of a túath occupied only the lowest rung on the ladder of Irish kingship. Kings possessed great might but limited power: They could lead their own people into battle, but could not normally command the troops drawn from other kingdoms; they could preside over the *oénach,* or local gathering of the túath, but issued legislation only in special circumstances, such as in times of war or plague. Nor, for that matter, did they own the tribal land they claimed as king; instead, they were farmers like everyone else, their wealth counted mostly in cattle and the number of acres they personally had under plow.

Kings of individual túatha existed within a loosely hierarchical structure of kingship. The law tracts distinguish two additional and higher grades of king: the *ruiri,* or "great king," who was not only king of his own túath but also overlord of three or four other túatha; and the *rí ruirech,* "king of overkings," who was king of a province. Yet the bonds between these kings and the tribes over which they ruled were personal and not institutional in nature. Submission was indicated by the exchange of hostages or tribute.

In the course of the eighth century, things began to change dramatically, as powerful rulers and families arose to challenge the traditional structure. The independence of individual túatha began to disappear as dynasties like the O'Neills began to exert their direct authority over the areas that they conquered. By Brian's time, many original túatha either had disappeared completely or had become so identified with the interests of the conquering king that the lesser rulers were no longer considered kings themselves but were called instead *tigerna,* "lord," or *tuísech,* "leader." (The modern variation, *taoiseach,* is the word for the prime minister of Ireland today.)

Brian was a beneficiary of these changes. The Dál Cais had originally been a weak and insignificant group with no claims to rule widely in Munster. However, the military acumen of Brian and his predecessors combined to put the Dál Cais on a different course. Ironically, one of the factors in Brian's rise was the presence in Ireland of the very Vikings that legend says he ousted forever from Ireland. Viking towns were a source of great wealth and military might: They could be powerful allies, or they could be raided and captured. Brian made use of them in every way possible, and his strategy paid off. Until his reign the position of ard-rí, or "high king," had been more of a theoretical possibility than an institutional reality. Brian changed all that.

For Brian Boru the years from 976 to 988 were more than eventful. In those dozen years he had ventured forth from the hills and woodlands of his native part of Munster to launch attacks into neighboring Leinster, Connacht, and Meath, killing when necessary, plundering when possible, and scooping up hostages as the circumstances allowed.

Brian was by no means the only one seeking to expand his kingdom during this time, however, and his exploits attracted the attention of the equally ambitious Máel Sechnaill II. King of Tara and head of the powerful O'Neill dynasty, Máel Sechnaill was determined to show his strength to the Munster king. In 982 he led forces from his own native Meath into the kingdom of Dál Cais, marched to the very spot where that túath inaugurated its kings, and in a flagrant act of provocation, cut down its sacred tree.

For the time being, Brian resisted any urge to retaliate. In fact, over the next couple of years the two kings continued to expand their own interests even as they kept a respectful distance from each other, Brian apparently believing that he was not yet a match for his Meath counterpart, and Máel Sechnaill not willing to put that belief to the test.

In the meantime, if the annals are to be

fleet, Brian launched his forces deep into Máel Sechnaill's kingdom. But the effects of the raid were short lived, and the following year the king of Tara evened the score with a foray into Munster. In this manner the two men crossed swords for years, one king's thrust blunted by the other's parry, until finally—having himself won the upper hand—Brian received word that Máel Sechnaill wanted to talk.

The two kings met in 997 near Clonfert in Connacht, opting, it would seem, for neutral ground lest either man be mistaken for having gone into the other's house and by that means submitted to his foe. Here, Brian Boru, deep now into his fifties but still with the flicker of blood lust in his eye, and Máel Sechnaill, 17 years the king of Tara and veteran himself of many a battle, fought as hard for a truce as they had for a victory. At length, a "mutual peace" was concluded, by the terms of which both men were to exchange hostages. In return, Máel Sechnaill

"Had I been able, I would have given you battle."

trusted, another, unexpected source of tension arose between the two kings. It came in the shape of an Irishwoman named Gormlaith. Queen Gormlaith had been the wife of a Viking named Amlaíb Cuaráin, who was then king of Dublin, and she was mother to their son, Sitriuc. Both beautiful and "utterly wicked," she was purportedly carried off by Máel Sechnaill in 980 and soon thereafter became his bride. Some five years later she is said to have abandoned her new husband and run off with yet another. That man was none other than Brian Boru.

By 988 Gormlaith's current husband and former husband were at war. Sailing up the Shannon River at the head of a great

was granted control of the northern half of Ireland "without war or trespass from Brian," while the Munster king was himself given a free hand in the south.

It was in exercising his dominion in the south of Ireland that Brian Boru trounced Sitriuc and Máel Mórda at Glen Máma two years later. Brian had never been more powerful. At last he had within grasp his ultimate goal, kingship of the whole island; in 1002 he marched against the king of Tara.

Some historians now believe that the climactic meeting between the two men took place at Athlone, where Máel Sechnaill had erected defenses on the Shannon in response to Brian's raiding. However, accounts written by Brian's descendants set the encounter not at Athlone but at the royal site of Tara. There, according to these sources, Máel Sechnaill nervously eyed the forces amassed against him and pondered again the choice Brian had given him: outright battle or immediate submission. Wisely, he stalled for time. A month's delay, Máel Sechnaill reasoned, should be enough time to gather an army that would have a fighting chance against so formidable a foe, and Brian, unwilling to take unfair advantage of the king of Tara, granted it.

As events turned out, the month's passage left the stalemate a stalemate. Having found no support among friends, Máel Sechnaill received little more from his O'Neill relatives. The O'Neills were no fools. "They knew," says one chronicle in explaining their response to the Munster threat, "that the Dál Cais would not retreat before them; and that they would not retreat before the Dál Cais; and they knew that it would

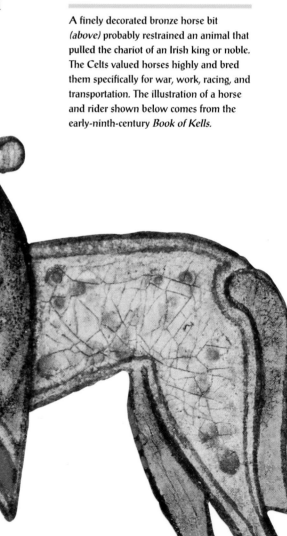

A finely decorated bronze horse bit *(above)* probably restrained an animal that pulled the chariot of an Irish king or noble. The Celts valued horses highly and bred them specifically for war, work, racing, and transportation. The illustration of a horse and rider shown below comes from the early-ninth-century *Book of Kells.*

be impossible to separate them, should they once join in battle, and that each would kill the other."

Máel Sechnaill was left with no choice. Erect on the back of his favorite mount, his face betraying none of the disappointment he felt, he set out for Brian's camp at Tara. Before and behind him rode some 200 horsemen, not a man among them sure of his safety save for his trust in his enemy's honor. Yet honor proved insurance enough, as the king and his cavalry entered the camp without incident and reined themselves to a stop in front of Brian's tent.

The clatter of hoofs and the snort of horses had drawn the attention of the Munster king, who stepped from his tent to see Máel Sechnaill. Stiffly but warmly, the two men greeted each other, then, pleasantries aside, got down to the business at hand, Máel Sechnaill coming immediately to the point. "Had I been able," he told Brian, "I would have given you battle." But, as he went on to explain, his eyes flecked with steel at the memory of the rebuff he'd received from his kinsmen, his inability to win the support of the O'Neills had left him with no option but to submit to Brian and to hand over hostages.

Spoiling perhaps for a fight, Brian was unwilling at first to accept Máel Sechnaill's surrender. Why not a truce, he suggested, his hands clasped, one thumb stroking the other; a yearlong truce, he added. Time enough to take an army north. Time enough for Brian to give those reluctant warriors, the O'Neills, the very battle they had tried so hard to avoid. Máel Sechnaill, eager to see the matter ended here and now, convinced him otherwise and

accepted Brian's gift of "twelve score steeds"—a number that matched the number of horsemen in his own retinue.

Like any such gift from victor to vanquished, this one was meant to confirm the latter's submission to the former. Máel Sechnaill well understood this, as did Brian. So, too, did every last rider in the king of Tara's retinue, each of whom now deigned to look his gift horse in the mouth and refuse it rather than acknowledge Brian's sovereignty. Thinking quickly lest he offend his host and jeopardize the deal, Máel Sechnaill immediately made a gift of all 240 horses to Brian's son Murchad. "They then parted in peace and with benedictions," says one source of the de facto Irish high king and the erstwhile king of Tara, now demoted to king of Meath, "and repaired to their respective homes."

Máel Sechnaill's submission to Brian Boru had brought one branch of the O'Neill clan into the fold. Displaying the same blend of courage and caution that had won him so much success in the past, the king of Munster bided his time, and then, after a couple of false starts, moved north in force and crushed the Ulster branch of the O'Neills. By 1006 he could declare himself what he had never doubted he would be: high king of Ireland.

His authority established, Brian now determined to make a circuit of his various subkingdoms, taking hostages from each to formally secure their submission. Upon his return, it would not have been out of character for the new ard-rí to order a feast to commemorate his victory, perhaps in a great banquet hall at his royal seat at Kincora, on the banks of the Shannon.

Brian's feast likely began with the sound of trumpets, as feasts did at Tara, whereupon the king and his invited subjects would have filed in and taken their allotted seats. Hundreds of guests were probably in attendance, along with the hundreds of cup-bearers, stewards, and footmen needed to keep the revelers supplied with food and drink. At some point in the festivities, one or more of the poets, or *filidh,* who formed part of Brian's ret-inue, would have sung the king's praises in poems composed es-pecially for the occasion. Typically, such poems traced the king's genealogy, and would certainly have lauded his wisdom and his prowess on the battlefield, as well as his physical perfection and manly vigor.

In addition to producing poetry on demand to suit a par-ticular occasion, the filidh were the living repositories of a túath's oral tradition. Accordingly, Brian and his guests could have ex-pected to hear one or more set pieces recounting the exploits of the legendary kings of Tara, foremost among them that most cel-ebrated of all Irish kings, Cormac Mac Airt. And so they un-doubtedly did on this occasion, as the appointed *fili* rose to em-broider the great Cormac's legend, even as the current king, Brian Boru, looked down from his dais on a scene that could only have cheered his warrior's heart—the air loud with laugh-ter and redolent with the honeyed scent of mead, tables heavy with half-eaten joints of meat, the hall itself aswim with cup-bearers scrambling to keep their charges well plied with drink. If generous hospitality was a measure of a king's honor, Brian may have mused, then this was certainly a feast worthy of Ire-land's new high king.

Turning his attention to the poet, Brian listened to the open-ing verses as the hall grew still. "From that day to this, there had never reigned a king so able and wise as Cormac," intoned the fili by way of a beginning, purposely leaving open the possibili-ty that King Brian might yet eclipse his predecessor. Then he went on to tell Cormac's story, beginning with his birth, a result of a tryst his father, King Airt, had had with a druid's daughter. "Lay with the king," the druid Olc Aiche had advised his beau-tiful daughter Achtán. "Lay with him, child, for good will come of it. Save what you bear he will leave no progeny, and the prog-eny that you bear will be kings of Ireland until doomsday."

Achtán had taken her father's words to heart, and nine months later she bore a son, whom she named Cormac. The druid Olc Aiche then fashioned five protective bands and placed them upon his infant grandson; the bands were to keep the boy forever safe from slaying and drowning, from fire and sorcery, and from attack by wolves.

Despite such precautions, however, the child had been whisked off by a she-wolf while his mother slept and was raised as another cub. In time, however, Cormac was rescued by a trap-per and eventually returned to his mother. Both then left for the north of Ireland, where Achtán placed her son in the care of Fíachnae Cassán, foster father of the boy's own father, who had himself recently been killed in battle.

Thirty years passed, and then Cormac, clad in his father's finest garments and carrying his father's sword at his side, set out on his own for Tara. Upon his arrival, he met a poor widow who confided to him her troubles. One of her sheep, she told him, had escaped into the queen's garden and stripped it of its veg-etables. As a result, the king, Lugaid Mac Con by name, had deemed her entire flock forfeit to the queen, and by that judg-ment deprived the widow of her livelihood. Taking up the dis-traught widow's case, Cormac confronted the king and accused him of poor judgment.

"And what," demanded Lugaid contemptuously, "would be thy just award?"

"My award would be that the wool of the sheep should pay for the vegetables the sheep has eaten," Cormac answered calmly, "because both the wool and the green things will grow again, and both parties will forget their hurt."

A shearing for a shearing, thought those in Lugaid's retinue that day. What could be fairer? And all there were left to wonder at the man's wisdom. Even old King Lugaid was taken aback, exclaiming in alarm, "It is the judgment of a king!" and sensing, as if told, that the stranger was the son of dead King Airt. One version of the tale says Cormac fled at once upon being recognized and returned to claim the throne for his own only after Lugaid was killed. Another version maintains that the king deferred to the superior judgment of the younger man: Proclaiming, "My time has come to an end," Lugaid abdicated on the spot.

The poet might have paused in his story at this point, if only to give his hearers a chance to top off their wooden mugs and himself a moment to wet his own throat. But one look around the hall would have told him that his audience needed no reminder of the message hidden in the story of Cormac and Lugaid. To a man, they all understood that no king was a good king unless he exercised what was known as *fír flathemon,* the "king's truth or justice."

Like the protective bands placed on Cormac by his druid grandfather, the king's truth was believed to ward off all manner of evils, not the least of them war, famine, and pestilence, so that guided by a just king the entire túath could expect peace and prosperity, good weather, and a rich abundance of crops. Such, it was said, was the Ireland of Cormac Mac Airt. "The world was full of every goodness in the time of that king," record the annals. "There was fruit of

tree and earth and sea. There was peace and ease and pleasure. There was neither slaughter nor reaving at that time, but everyone in his own ancestral place."

On the other hand, the reign of an unjust king would be marked by enough calamities to warrant his removal from office. In one version of the story of Cormac and Lugaid, the latter remained king for a year after his misguided judgment on the widow, during which time "grass did not come through the earth nor a leaf through trees nor grain into corn." The solution was obvious to his subjects. "Then the men of Ireland expelled him from his kingship," the sagas declare, "because he was a false king."

Picking up the thread of his poem, the fili continued his tale. The noble Cormac, he avowed, would never have behaved as Lugaid had. Instead, Cormac had been exemplary in ways that the majority of men are merely ordinary and had been in every respect "handsome, fair, without blemish, without defect." He exhibited the time-honored traits of the ideal king, a list that ran the gamut from merciful, righteous, and proper to firm, generous, hospitable, and well spoken.

A good thing, too, since Irish kingship was a sacral kingship, one that demanded that its foremost representative be perfect in body and sterling in virtue. Any physical defect, no less than a flaw in judg-

tara of the kings

At first sight it appears unremarkable, a wind-swept grassy hill rising just over 500 feet above sea level and little more than 300 feet above the surrounding countryside. It features no castles or great buildings, just a collection of mounds, banks, and ditches, and several large stones. But although the location seems lacking in grandeur, no place else captures Ireland's royal past like *Temair na Ríg,* or "Tara of the Kings."

From its rounded summit one can begin to appreciate the qualities of Tara. Perched on the Plain of Meath, it overlooks some of the most fertile pasture land in all of Europe, land that stretches for miles in every direction. Its scenic panorama is matched only by the great sweeping view that Tara provides into the history of Ireland, a story that has often unfolded on and around this ancient hill.

According to legend, the divine Túatha Dé Danaan invaded Ireland several thousand years ago. After defeating a tribe called the Fomhoire,

they ruled from Tara, and forever after the hill would be known as the seat of kings. When the first Celts arrived in Ireland they, too, were drawn to Tara. On top of the hill they discovered an ancient burial mound; identifying the site in their own cosmology as an entrance to the otherworld, the Celts made Tara a sacred place. Every year the kings of Celtic Ireland would gather there to mark the beginning of winter.

Over the centuries many great names in Irish history have been associated with Tara. The legendary third-century king Cormac Mac Airt was said by medieval storytellers to have built a royal residence and an expansive banquet hall at Tara and kept his captives at a site on the hill known as the Mound of Hostages. Saint Patrick is believed to have come to Tara to confront Irish paganism and challenge directly the power of the druids. And when the mighty O'Neill clan sought to extend their power, they did so by laying claim to the kingship of Tara.

Any man who would rule at Tara, the sagas claimed, had to pass four tests before becoming king. He had to mount the

This stone, perhaps the original *Lia Fáil* coronation stone, stands in one of the ancient circular ramparts that crown the Hill of Tara *(far left).*

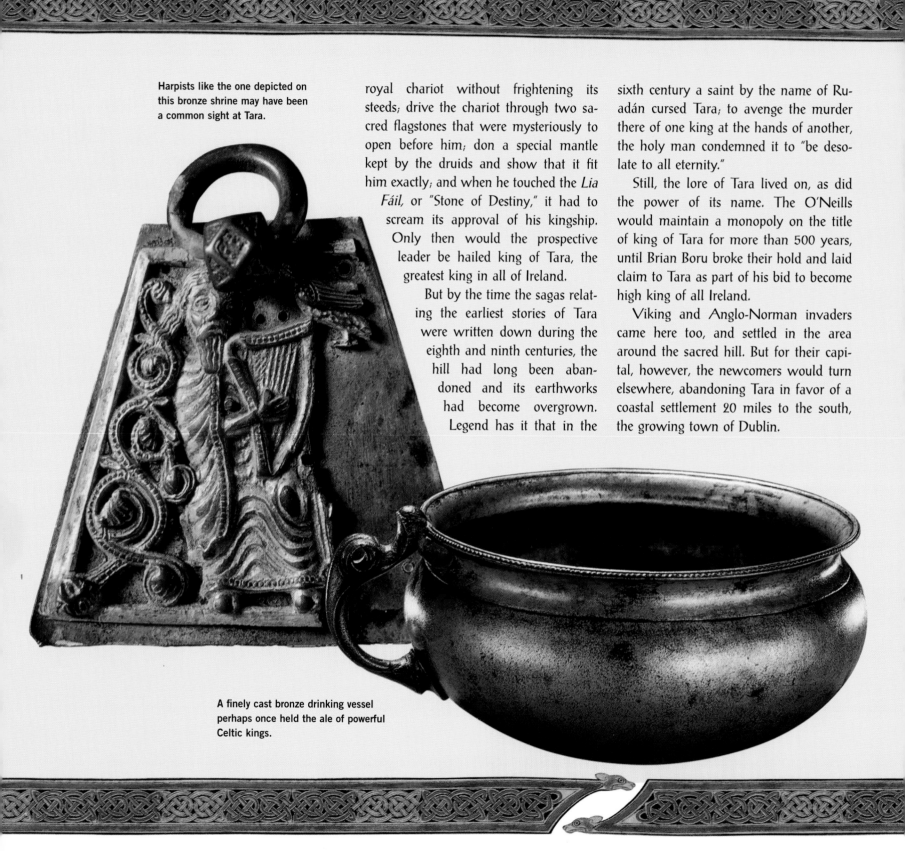

Harpists like the one depicted on this bronze shrine may have been a common sight at Tara.

A finely cast bronze drinking vessel perhaps once held the ale of powerful Celtic kings.

royal chariot without frightening its steeds; drive the chariot through two sacred flagstones that were mysteriously to open before him; don a special mantle kept by the druids and show that it fit him exactly; and when he touched the *Lia Fáil,* or "Stone of Destiny," it had to scream its approval of his kingship. Only then would the prospective leader be hailed king of Tara, the greatest king in all of Ireland.

But by the time the sagas relating the earliest stories of Tara were written down during the eighth and ninth centuries, the hill had long been abandoned and its earthworks had become overgrown. Legend has it that in the

sixth century a saint by the name of Ruadán cursed Tara; to avenge the murder there of one king at the hands of another, the holy man condemned it to "be desolate to all eternity."

Still, the lore of Tara lived on, as did the power of its name. The O'Neills would maintain a monopoly on the title of king of Tara for more than 500 years, until Brian Boru broke their hold and laid claim to Tara as part of his bid to become high king of all Ireland.

Viking and Anglo-Norman invaders came here too, and settled in the area around the sacred hill. But for their capital, however, the newcomers would turn elsewhere, abandoning Tara in favor of a coastal settlement 20 miles to the south, the growing town of Dublin.

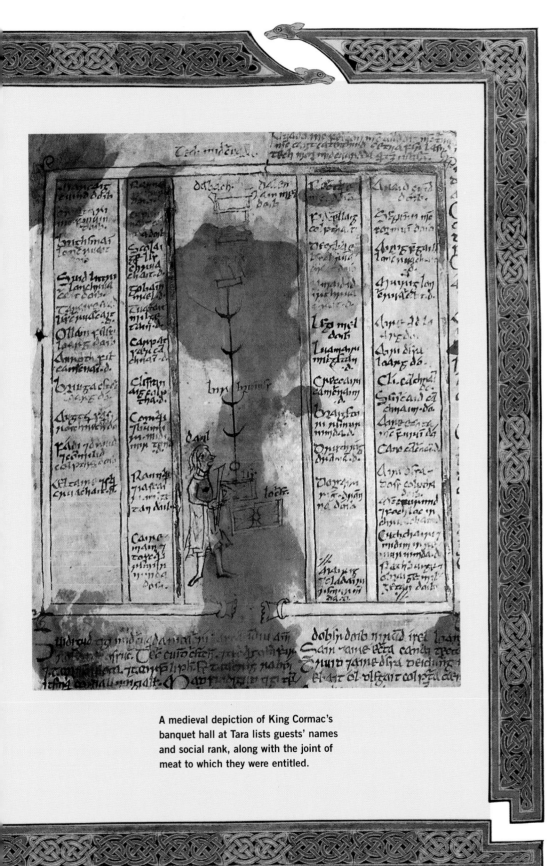

A medieval depiction of King Cormac's banquet hall at Tara lists guests' names and social rank, along with the joint of meat to which they were entitled.

ment, was theoretically cause for a king's dethronement, which explains why one seventh-century king of Tara was said to have been deposed after he was blinded in one eye by a bee. Unluckier still were those kings who were unseated when they were intentionally mutilated—blinding and castration being the preferred means of disfigurement—at the hands of rivals to the throne. And although the outright murder of a king or his heir apparent supposedly barred the murderer from kingship, in practice many a man guilty of king slaying appears to have stepped to power over the corpse of his predecessor.

The poet would have gone on to tell of how Cormac was inaugurated as king of Tara, in a ceremony that symbolized the marriage of the king to the goddess of the land. Such unions were believed to ensure the fertility of the kingdom and its people. According to a later chronicler, there were some kings among the northern O'Neills who took the consummation of these unions all too literally, by mating with a white mare in full view of their subjects. "The mare is then killed immediately," wrote Gerald of Wales in the late 12th century, "cut up in pieces, and boiled in water." The new king bathed in this broth, again in front of a crowd, while dining on the horse's boiled flesh and lapping up the same broth in which he bobbed. "When this unrighteous rite has

Two images from the manuscript of Gerald of Wales, *The History and Topography of Ireland,* illustrate the coronation ritual in which a king-elect sacrifices a white mare and cooks it in a cauldron *(below);* the new king then bathes in the animal's broth and shares its flesh with his subjects *(right).*

been carried out," concluded Gerald, "his kingship and dominion have been conferred."

Like other kings, Cormac would have been subject to a detailed set of restrictions. Some of these impositions were designed to ensure that a king behaved at all times in accordance with the dignity of his office. He could not, for example, use a spade or an ax, common tools meant to be used by commoners. And lest he offend the gods and court misfortune, he had to be forever mindful of a whole host of taboos. "You shall not pass Tara on your right hand and Brega on your left," warned one such taboo. "You shall not stay abroad from Tara for nine nights; and you shall not spend the night in a house from which firelight is visible outside after sunset and into which one can see from outside."

His poem done at last, the fili threaded his way to his seat through aisles suddenly choked with Brian Boru's warriors, their cheeks flushed with mead, swords jangling at their sides. Each of these battle-hardened men would have been careful to treat the fili with respect, however. As a class, poets often wielded as much influence as a king, especially when it came to the shaping of public opinion. Moreover, they were thought to have supernatural powers, so that nobody, not even the king, stepped afoul of a fili without fear of the consequences.

The power of the filidh notwithstanding, it was the king who ruled the roost in Irish society, although he was by no means omnipotent, restrained as he was by an ancient and highly developed legal code and by that formidable learned class of poets and druids. Kingship was not an administrative or bureaucratic position. Rather, it was very much a festive office in which the king performed a variety of roles, from the provision of hospitality, fertility, and justice to leadership in war and prowess at the hunt. In all that he did, he had always to *act* like a king.

And that role was prescribed by law. According to one eighth-century law tract on kingship, for instance, Sunday was

than on long, drawn-out campaigns. And having fought to claim the high kingship, Brian now had to fight in order to defend it from those who would take it away. At no time in the first decade of the 11th century could he let down his guard, as would-be usurpers repeatedly challenged his authority. More worrisome still, by 1012, old and frail at 71, he had the beginnings of an all-out revolt on his hands.

Later accounts assert that Brian owed his most recent troubles to the irrepressible Gormlaith. He and Gormlaith had been divorced since the year 995, but of late she had been breathing fire into her brother Máel Mórda, king of Leinster, by rubbing his nose into his subservience to her former husband. "Did your father submit to Brian's father," she had upbraided Máel Mórda, "or your grandfather to Brian's grandfather? Of course not, for they were men, unlike you. And now, no doubt, Brian's son will trample upon your son, just as Brian tramples upon you!"

Her words were still smoldering the next day, when Brian's son Murchad added insult to injury, after a run-in over a game of chess, by reminding the already slighted Máel Mórda of the time he had been caught hiding in a yew tree after the Battle of Glen Máma. Máel Mórda bristled at the put-down and steamed off vowing to avenge his own wounded pride. Casting the affront to himself as an insult to all of Leinster, he persuaded his fellow Leinstermen to withdraw their submission to Brian and Gormlaith's son, Sitriuc, to do the same. So it was that a dozen

reserved for drinking ale, "for he is no rightful prince who does not promise ale for every Sunday; Monday for legal business, for adjudicating between túatha; Tuesday for chess; Wednesday for watching greyhounds hunting; Thursday for marital intercourse; Friday for horseracing; Saturday for judgments." And during the heroic age of long ago that was described in the epic *Táin Bó Cuailnge*—"The Cattle Raid of Cooley"—the hours of the day were ordained. Ulster's King Connor spent "a third of the day watching [his foster] boys, another third playing chess, and another third drinking ale until sleep overtakes him."

But the kingship of Brian Boru was not the kingship of Cormac Mac Airt, as Brian himself well knew. Gone were the days when a man might rise to power, as Cormac supposedly had, by dint of his wisdom rather than by force of arms. Gone, too, were the days when warfare amounted to little more than raiding, with its emphasis on the theft of cattle and the taking of hostages rather years after Brian had defeated them at Glen Máma, the kings of Leinster and Dublin were in open rebellion once again.

The following year, 1013, Brian's men ravaged Leinster, and by September he had reached the walls of Dublin. From then until Christmas his forces laid siege to the city, at which point Brian ordered them to break camp and return home with neither a victory nor a single hostage to show for their efforts.

The defenders of Dublin knew better than to relax, however. Wasting no time, Sitriuc and Máel Mórda set about securing the assistance of their Norse and Irish kinsmen. Sitriuc himself went to the earl of the Orkney Islands to cement an alliance, supposedly in return for his mother's hand in marriage and the kingship of Dublin upon the successful outcome of the battle. He then sailed to the Isle of Man, where he tendered the same request—and made the same promise—to a lapsed Viking Christian named Brodir; Brodir and his Norsemen were to be enlisted, Gormlaith had firmly instructed her son, "whatever the conditions they demand."

By Palm Sunday of 1014 Sitriuc may have thought that he had gotten much more than he might ever have reckoned on. Vikings said to number in the thousands had risen in response to his entreaties, and their ships now crowded Dublin Bay and the sandy shores of the Liffey River. A thousand or more may have sailed with Brodir alone, every last man sheathed from head to foot in the strongest armor of polished iron or gleaming brass. More reportedly came from the Orkneys, and more still from France, Wales, Scotland, and the Hebrides. To these, Máel Mórda added the three battalions he had mustered in Ireland itself, so that in the end there were seven great battalions prepared to do battle with the forces of King Brian Boru.

Though weighed down with age, Brian would not be caught napping. The ard-rí had assembled warriors from all over Munster and Connacht, as well as the army of Meath, under the leadership of Máel Sechnaill. Together they marched again on Dublin, burning and pillaging at every opportunity, their fires signposting their advance and alerting the defenders of the city of their approach. When at last flames were seen leaping from the hills just north of Dublin, the Norsemen and their Leinster allies could contain themselves no longer. They marched forth to attack Brian's army.

Whether the sky was blue or gray on that Good Friday morning in 1014 is lost to memory, whether the air hung close or was stirred by breezes has gone unmentioned. But the dreams of men the previous night had been disturbed by all manner of portents and visions on the eve of the battle history records as Clontarf. Brodir, for one, imagined himself and his men scalded by a rain of boiling blood and scavenged by flocks of ravens whose beaks and talons seemed made of iron. Far away in Scotland, another Viking claimed to have seen a woman weaving entrails at a loom weighted with the severed heads of men. Nor was the sleep of Brian's men any sounder. Some from his native Dál Cais dreamed of a fairy woman foretelling disaster. Others dreamed of dead monks demanding compensation for a long-ago raid on their monastery; when asked to wait until tomorrow for the money due them, the monks replied, ominously, that tomorrow would be too late.

From the plain of Magh n-Elda, according to later tracts, Brian looked out upon a sea of his advancing warriors, "and beheld the battle phalanx, compact, huge, disciplined, moving in silence, mutely, bravely, haughtily, unitedly, with one mind, traversing the plain towards them; and three score and ten banners over them, of red, and of yellow, and of green, and of all kinds of colors." Spears glittered above their heads, shields were held protectively across their bodies, and axes and swords were readied "for hewing and for hacking, for maiming and mutilating skins, and bodies, and skulls."

This great army was without the soldiers of Máel Sechnaill,

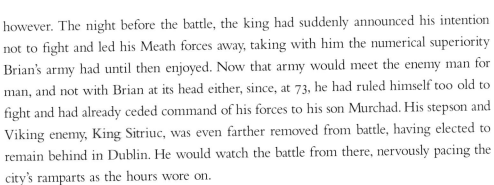

LEISURE TIME

This tiny figure of a queen *(below, right)*, of carved ivory or polished bone, once traversed the chessboard of an Irish nobleman of the 1100s. Wearing a crown and seated on a high-backed throne, she holds her hand to her cheek as if contemplating her master's next move. Should the nobleman tire of chess, he might amuse himself instead with a peg game such as the one shown at right, which may be of Viking origin.

The sons of Irish kings and nobles did not spend all their time at play; they were taught to swim, ride, hunt, and fight, all pursuits considered appropriate for men of rank. Girls of comparable social standing learned to run a household while perfecting the arts of weaving, embroidery, and needlework.

however. The night before the battle, the king had suddenly announced his intention not to fight and led his Meath forces away, taking with him the numerical superiority Brian's army had until then enjoyed. Now that army would meet the enemy man for man, and not with Brian at its head either, since, at 73, he had ruled himself too old to fight and had already ceded command of his forces to his son Murchad. His stepson and Viking enemy, King Sitriuc, was even farther removed from battle, having elected to remain behind in Dublin. He would watch the battle from there, nervously pacing the city's ramparts as the hours wore on.

"And then ensued a conflict," writes one account of the battle, "wrestling, wounding, noisy, bloody, crimsoned, terrible, fierce, quarrelsome." Through the morning and all through the afternoon, the battle raged, the clash of arms, the crush of bodies, the smashing of skulls echoing from cliff to cavern and tree to tree, the wind at one point streaming blood and hair. Early on, tall, strong Brodir, clad in armor "that no weapon could pierce," his long black hair tucked under his belt, had led his chain-mailed warriors into the fray, scything the field of all who dared oppose them. But by day's end, it was Brodir's Vikings and the men of Leinster who were in full retreat, scurrying as fast as panicked legs could carry them, praying their way back to Dublin and the ships they had left beached at sunrise.

As the first of the Norsemen reached the northern shore of Dublin Bay they saw to their alarm that the tide had refloated their ships and had carried them out to sea. Worse still, they found that a detachment of Brian's troops had maneuvered around their flank and was now between them and the safety of the city. There was now only one way out. "They retreated therefore to the sea," reads the chronicle, "like a herd of cows in heat, from sun, and from gadflies, and from insects." Pursued into the waves by Brian's forces, many were slaughtered and many more, weighted in armor, drowned in the bloody froth of the sea, so that "they lay in heaps and in hundreds, confounded, after parting with their bodily senses and understandings."

Only a few of the Vikings escaped. Among them was Brodir, slashing his way through the Irish ranks and plunging into the spring-green sanctuary of a nearby forest. Moving as stealthily as men in armor could move, he and two companions

a time for heroes

When kings and chieftains of early Ireland retired to their great halls in the evening, they would call upon their poets and court musicians to provide some entertainment. Accompanying themselves on harps similar to the one at left, the performers sang tales of days of old—of gods and magic, of wondrous beasts and superhuman men, of warfare and quests and the heroes of ancient Ireland.

Many of these elements are represented in the stories known as the Ulster Cycle, which tells of that province's powerful king, Connor Mac Nessa, and his struggles with neighboring Connacht. To defend his borders, Connor called on a band of fearless warriors, the most famous of whom was the mighty Cu Chulainn.

Described as the bravest warrior in Ireland, Cu Chulainn was the model mythical champion. His otherworld father was said to be the god Lugh, from whom he gained supernatural powers. When in battle, for example, a terrible transformation took place: His muscles swelled, his body shook beneath his skin, one eye protruded from his head while the other sank into his skull, and a golden glow known as the hero light shone around his head.

Cu Chulainn's valor is celebrated in the central tale of the Ulster Cycle, the epic *Táin Bó Cuailnge,* or "The Cattle Raid of Cooley." The tale starts with a quarrel between Maeve, the queen of Connacht, and her consort, Ailill, over whose possessions were superior. Comparing their properties, they found the score was even, except for one thing: Ailill owned a great white bull whose power and ferocity were matched only by Ulster's brown bull of Cooley. Maeve was determined to have the brown bull, and when her requests for it were rebuffed, she raised an army from all over Ireland to seize the beast by force.

As a result of a curse from the goddess Macha, the warriors of Ulster were stricken with a mysterious sickness that came upon them in times of crisis. So as Maeve's forces crossed into the province, Connor and his men could not take to the field of battle—all except Cu Chulainn. Being of divine blood, he had escaped Macha's curse.

Irish poets loved to tell how all Ireland was embroiled in a battle that started over a cattle raid for a bull such as this one, which illustrates a 12th-century manuscript.

Mounting his chariot alongside his charioteer, Lóeg, Cu Chulainn went off to meet Maeve's army as Ulster's sole defender.

Day after day he harassed the invading force, slaughtering its scouts and outriders and leaving their bloody heads spiked on the branches of trees. At night, Cu Chulainn would ride his chariot right into the enemies' camps, his sword slashing, the champion's battle fury upon him and the golden glow of the hero light about his head.

Hundreds of Maeve's men died. It was said that some perished of fright at the very sight of the Ulsterman: His hair stood on end, his body trembled, and from his gaping mouth came a terrible howl that caused all the local spirits to howl with him.

Eventually, Macha's curse began to lift, and King Connor and the warriors of Ulster came to the support of Cu Chulainn. The Connacht army broke ranks and fled. In the chaos that ensued, Queen Maeve seized the brown bull of Cooley and drove it off with her retreating army.

The brown bull cried three mighty bellows when he saw the strange land of Connacht, and Ailill's white bull immediately came to challenge him. All day and all night the two animals fought, chasing each other across Ireland. By morning Ailill's bull was dead, impaled on the horns of the brown bull. Victorious, the brown bull bounded back to Ulster, but when he came to Cooley his great heart burst with bellowing and he fell dead.

Maeve could never forgive Cu Chulainn for the humiliating defeat he had given her, and seven years later she led another army back to the borders of Ulster. Among the army's ranks were two warriors named Lugaid and Erc, whose fathers had been killed by Cu Chulainn. The pair enlisted the help of a group of sorcerers, who fashioned three magical spears, each of which, it was prophesied, would kill a king.

As this new crisis loomed, the old curse disabled the warriors of Ulster, and once again Cu Chulainn and his trusty charioteer rode off to stop the enemy alone. This

Bound to a rock, Cu Chulainn dies facing his enemies, who can tell by the crow on his shoulder that the Ulsterman is close to death.

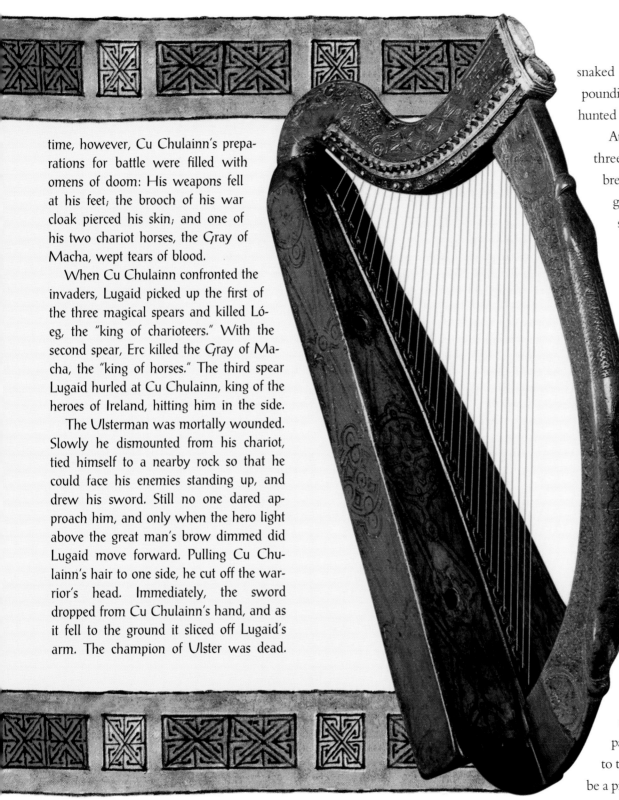

time, however, Cu Chulainn's preparations for battle were filled with omens of doom: His weapons fell at his feet; the brooch of his war cloak pierced his skin; and one of his two chariot horses, the Gray of Macha, wept tears of blood.

When Cu Chulainn confronted the invaders, Lugaid picked up the first of the three magical spears and killed Ló-eg, the "king of charioteers." With the second spear, Erc killed the Gray of Macha, the "king of horses." The third spear Lugaid hurled at Cu Chulainn, king of the heroes of Ireland, hitting him in the side.

The Ulsterman was mortally wounded. Slowly he dismounted from his chariot, tied himself to a nearby rock so that he could face his enemies standing up, and drew his sword. Still no one dared approach him, and only when the hero light above the great man's brow dimmed did Lugaid move forward. Pulling Cu Chulainn's hair to one side, he cut off the warrior's head. Immediately, the sword dropped from Cu Chulainn's hand, and as it fell to the ground it sliced off Lugaid's arm. The champion of Ulster was dead.

snaked through the woods, hearts pounding, eyes wide with fear, the hunted outrunning the hunters.

At the edge of a clearing the three men paused to catch their breath and peered out from the greenery. Somewhat to their surprise, they saw a tent in the clearing and, kneeling inside, a white-haired man, prayer book in hand, his safety ensured by a ring of warriors forming a shield wall.

What happened next depends on who tells the tale. As a Norse saga has it, Brodir watched for a moment, slowly realizing the part destiny had given him to play and suddenly mindful of his good fortune. The old man had to be King Brian, he thought to himself, one hand already tightening on the hilt of his sword as he broke from the forest and rushed the king's guard. Yet the Irish account has Brodir and his companions walking past the tent, paying little heed to the kneeling figure they took to be a priest, even as Brian himself rose

A modern lithograph depicts the Viking warrior Brodir overpowering a young bodyguard in order to smite the Irish high king, Brian Boru. Brian's death at the Battle of Clontarf was a tragedy for the Munster forces and a major setback for the fortunes of his descendants, the O'Briens.

and unsheathed his sword at this unexpected threat. "Brodir passed him by and noticed him not," says the chronicle, until one of his two companions, a man who had once served in Brian's army, recognized the old man for the king he was. Brodir spun on his heels, sword in hand.

Whatever the circumstances, the outcome was the same. The three Vikings managed to breach the shield wall, and Brodir raced for the tent, his weapon wet with the blood of the king's guard. "When Brian saw him," goes the Irish story, "he gazed at him, and gave him a stroke with his sword, and cut off his left leg at the knee, and his right leg at the foot." Brodir, bleeding, drew a great breath, then parted the air with a mighty swing of his

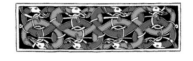

many as 19,000 men may have been struck down in a single day, among them most of the kings and chieftains of both sides, Sitriuc alone having survived by the good fortune of having remained behind in Dublin.

But Donncadh was no Brian Boru, and in the wake of his father's death he and his kinsmen had trouble enough maintaining control of Munster and no hope at all of retaining the high kingship. Instead, Máel Sechnaill re-claimed his position as the most powerful king in Ireland and held it until 1022, when death at last claimed him. New dynasties then arose to vie with one another for the high kingship, among them the O'Connors, the Mac Murroughs, and the Mac Loughlins, clans who formed

"The nun herself was carried off a prisoner and put into a man's bed."

sword, cleaving the old king's head from his body with a single stroke. His deed done, the Irish account claims, Brian's slayer turned to await his own end, he and the other two Vikings going down in a swarm of Irish warriors. In the Norse version, Brodir remained defiant to the end, yelling out, "Let the word go round that Brodir has felled King Brian," before being cut down by the royal bodyguards.

Not until the evening of Easter Sunday did Donncadh, son of Brian and Gormlaith, return from a raid on Leinster to retrieve his father's body and to claim the standard of kingship, his half brother Murchad having also died in the battle. And not until then did Donncadh fathom the full horror of Clontarf, where the field was sown with discarded weapons, and the harvest of the dead and dying lay on the earth like so many toppled sheaves. As

and broke alliances as easily as they bore and buried grudges.

At the same time the whole notion of warfare was changing. Increasingly, kings were mounting prolonged and bloody campaigns that dragged on for months, settling little for long and mostly setting the stage for further campaigns. Kingship, too, became more militarized in the 11th century, as castles rose where none had been, professional standing armies came to replace the recruits of old, and kings built and maintained their own naval fleets. The effect was to render the entire island, as the annalists wrote of 12th-century Ireland, "a trembling sod."

But if the goal of all this saber-rattling was still the high kingship, it remained a prize as slippery as it had ever been, though one made all the more desirable once Brian Boru had shown that a single man could indeed rule the island of Ireland. In the century and a half after Brian's death there was never any shortage of contenders for the prize, and none was more determined than the handsome king of Leinster, Dermot Mac Murrough, who muscled his way onto the stage of Irish politics in the mid-12th century.

Born around the year 1110, Dermot had been weaned on the great Irish epics and found in the exploits of his country's mythical heroes the inspiration for his own kingly aspirations. At the age of 16 he was the king of his own túath, and he set out with a vengeance to realize those aspirations—namely, to return his native province to its ancient greatness and eventually to procure for himself the high kingship of Ireland.

By his early twenties Dermot had established himself as king of Leinster, attaining the provincial throne after defeating the challenge of a rival dynasty. But before he could embark on loftier endeavors, Dermot first had to secure the loyalty of the trading towns of Wexford and Waterford and then restore Leinster to the boundaries of the previous century by extending his kingdom west toward the Shannon and north to Dublin. That done, he had to choose sides in the dynastic wars that had swept Ireland in the early 1140s—and had to hope that he made the right choice. Holding a finger to the prevailing political wind, he opted to join forces with Ulster's Muirchertach Mac Loughlin, who was soon to be high king, thus setting himself up against Turlough O'Connor, the king of Connacht and would-be high king, and his ally Tigernán O'Rourke, a king of Meath.

Kindness was not necessarily a virtue in the power politics of the time, and while Dermot later made amends for his excesses by establishing churches and convents in his kingdom, he also earned himself a reputation for abject ruthlessness. Long after the wounds had healed, for example, people still talked about how Dermot had once put down a revolt in north Leinster by having 17 of its local chieftains blinded. And to his dying day, few of his enemies ever whispered the name of Dermot Mac Murrough without dredging up the memory of the abbess of Saint Brigit's in Kildare, whose misfortune it was to be a member of a rival dynasty. On Dermot's orders in 1132, say the annals, "the nun herself was carried off a prisoner and put into a man's bed."

Abduction was also the order of the day in 1152 when Dermot earned himself the undying enmity of Tigernán O'Rourke by carrying off his wife. How much a part the beautiful Derbforgaill played in her own kidnapping is open to conjecture, but as the story goes, Dermot may have been feeling his oats at the age of 42 when he set his

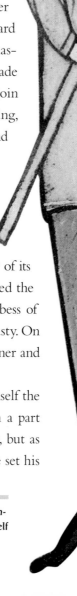

Desperate to re-claim the kingship of Leinster, Dermot Mac Murrough allied himself with the Anglo-Normans.

sights on the wife of his rival. Her own blushing maidenhood long behind her at 44, Derbforgaill may well have incited her suitor to act, since some say she sent Dermot a message to that effect. But in any case Dermot wasted no time in saddling up and galloping off to her "rescue" at the head of a detachment of cavalry. Upon reaching his distressed damsel, "he ordered that she be placed on horseback behind a rider," wrote one historian from the 17th century, "and upon this the woman wept and screamed in pretense, as if Dermot were carrying her off by force, and bringing her with him in this fashion, he returned to Leinster."

Dermot may well have had more than romance on his mind when he absconded with Derbforgaill, however, since stealing a man's wife was an even greater insult to him than stealing his cattle (which Dermot had also done). But if Dermot bedded Derbforgaill at all, he did so only for a year before the faithless wife reconciled with her husband Tigernán and returned home. Not one to forgive and forget, the cuckolded Meath king plotted revenge and struck back the following year by plundering part of Dermot's kingdom.

The success of this foray must have pleased Tigernán without quite satisfying him. Still, he could be as patient as his enemy was ruthless, and if it took him a lifetime, he was determined to get even with Dermot for the harm done to his honor.

As it was, it took 14 years. In 1166, after the death of his ally, the ard-rí Muirchertach Mac Loughlin—and the inevitable free-for-all for the high kingship that followed—Dermot found himself on the wrong side of a fearsome alliance that included the new high king, Rory O'Connor, son of the by now dead Turlough, and the embittered Tigernán O'Rourke. Following an uprising against Dermot by the Norse of Dublin and several prominent north Leinster families, the opportunist Tigernán decided to act. With the blessing of O'Connor, Tigernán and his forces swooped down on Leinster, marched into the very heart of Dermot's kingdom, and demolished his fortress. Dermot him-

Too busy with his own territories to lead an invasion himself, Henry II allowed his red-and-gold standard—similar to the one shown above—to be carried into Ireland.

self was ousted from his kingship and, with too many foes in pursuit and too few friends in support, soon took passage across the Irish Sea for England.

Dermot Mac Murrough in England was a king without a kingdom and desperate to have it back. With a fair wind behind him, he had arrived in Bristol in August 1166, in the company of his wife, their daughter Eva, and a small entourage of followers, and had no sooner settled in at the home of a friend when he hit upon a plan that would make uneasy bedfellows of his native Ireland and neighboring England.

It had occurred to Dermot that just a year earlier he had given the Norman king of England, Henry II, the loan of his Dublin fleet so that Henry could lean the more on his own rebellious Welsh subjects. Dermot figured that the debt had come due and that Henry could be of equal use to him in re-claiming his own kingdom. Finding the peripatetic king was no easy matter, however, since Henry had the habit of wandering a domain that embraced not only England but much of France. Having searched first for him in Normandy, Dermot headed next for the south of France, inquiring in city after city for the wayward king.

Sometime after Christmas, Dermot finally caught up to Henry in Aquitaine in the southwest of the country, and there he made his case for the English monarch's help. "May God who dwells on high ward and save you, King Henry," croaked the once and future king of Leinster, the hoarseness of his voice, it was said, the result of having too often shouted above the din of battle. He had

come, Dermot continued, in order to avenge the shame wrought upon him by his own people. What had been done to him was wrong, he argued as he fumbled nervously with the belt around his tunic. "No king should ever be cast from his kingdom," he declared—"*no* king," calculating that his words would bring a nod of agreement from a fellow ruler.

Henry, ruddy in complexion and paunchy already at 34, was sympathetic but unwilling as yet to make any commitments. Nobody needed to remind him that he had his own troubles. Those ever-recalcitrant Welsh, for example. That obstinate bishop, Becket. An insurrection brewing in Brittany and another right here in Aquitaine. Not to mention those damnable Scots. And as much as he would have loved to have a hand in Ireland—and better yet a hand *on* Ireland—that country was not yet ripe for the plucking.

All this, however, the English king kept to himself as Dermot humbled himself even further in an effort to secure Henry's support. "To you I come to make plaint, good sire, in the presence of the barons of your empire," Dermot pleaded, hoping that the gray-eyed king and his coterie of linened lords would take his obeisance for sincerity. "Hear, noble King Henry," he started, then paused, catching himself momentarily before promising what he never wanted to promise any man: "Your liegeman I shall become henceforth all the days of my life," he vowed, "on condition that you be my helper."

Henry stopped a smile. What to do. Here was opportunity, albeit one that would have its price in blood, and while he was not squeamish about the use of force, he dared not risk his already stretched

Portrayed in battle on his seal, Strongbow used the might of his sword to bring him wealth, land, and title in Ireland.

Dermot gives his daughter Eva to the mercenary Strongbow in a marriage that forever linked the Irish and the Anglo-Normans.

A FOREIGN KING

In 1171 King Henry II of England crossed the Irish Sea with a well-equipped army to assert his royal mastery over both the Irish and those Anglo-Normans inclined to view themselves as independent lieges rather than vassals of the Crown.

During his triumphant tour of the country, Henry visited the cathedral atop the Rock of Cashel *(left)*, ancient seat of the kings of Munster, in order to accept a pledge of fealty from Irish bishops. Before leaving Ireland, the king declared Dublin the capital of his colonial administration and issued the city its first municipal charter *(right)*.

forces. What to do, he pondered, pacing a few steps away from his royal supplicant, his hands clenched loosely behind his broad back. What on earth to do.

It made no sense, of course, to send the Irish king on his way, the calculating Henry thought to himself. Dermot might seek help elsewhere, among the Scots, for example, and no good could ever come of that. And then there was Ireland itself. What king wouldn't want that gem as a jewel in his crown. And didn't he have a right to Ireland, anyway? The pope himself had said as much a decade earlier in a document that at once confirmed the church's ownership of all the world's islands—and deeded Ireland to the English king. Perhaps, then, something could be done. Perhaps, the ever-scheming Henry reasoned, by assisting Dermot now, with his left hand as it were, he could leave open the possibility of taking a firmer grip with the right at another, more opportune moment in the future.

Turning again to Dermot, Henry accepted the Irish king's fealty and promised him what help he could. Dermot brightened, and brightened all the more when Henry weighed him down with gifts before his departure and, more to the point, with letters bearing the English king's sign and seal and giving "Dermot, Prince of Leinster," the right to raise a private army. "Wherefore," the document proclaimed in part, "whosoever within the bounds of our territories shall be willing to give him aid, as our vassal and liegeman, in recovering his dominion, let him be assured of our favor and license in that behalf."

With Henry's sanction to do what needed to be done, Dermot retraced his path to England and soon set about recruiting an army. He found few takers at first, even after sweetening the offer with promises of land and money, until at length he had the good fortune to meet the red-haired and freckled earl of Strigiul, Richard Fitz-Gilbert, a man whose thin voice and feminine face belied his strapping nickname, Strongbow. But the patrician Strongbow—"whose past was brighter than his prospects," wrote the historian Gerald of Wales, "whose blood was better than his brains"—had his own reasons for agreeing to be part of the venture and his own conditions as well: He wanted to succeed Dermot as king of Leinster upon the Irishman's death, and to confirm the arrangement, he demanded the hand of Dermot's daughter Eva in marriage.

For better or worse, Dermot agreed to Strongbow's demands. Next, he set out for Wales, where he had no trouble rounding up recruits to his cause—a band of Norman adventurers, Flemish mercenaries, and Welsh insurgents, all of whom had been hardened by years of fighting in Wales and were eager to hone their skills further in Ireland and at the same time win land

by paying Tigernán 100 ounces of gold as compensation for his long-ago abduction of Derbforgaill, then so be it. Anything, so long as he maintained his foothold in Ireland.

His pride restored and his eyes aglitter with gold, Tigernán obviously thought that he had Dermot at bay. But he had let the snake into his midst, and coiled and hissing, Dermot awaited his opportunity to strike. A year later, in 1168, the annals record, "a large body of knights came overseas to Mac Murrough." Shortly thereafter, Dermot and this second and stronger contingent of mercenaries laid siege to Wexford, the opening salvo in an all-out effort to win back Leinster. By the autumn of 1169, not only Leinster but Dublin owed allegiance to Dermot, who now wrote to Strongbow in Wales, urging him to make haste for Ireland. Months passed, and then, in August 1170, the horizon south of Waterford

" . . . whose past was brighter than his prospects, whose blood was better than his brains."

for themselves. Dermot had few doubts that these men could do the job, and confident of success, he put his back to the sea-gnawed coast of Wales and shoved off for Ireland.

In the annals of Ireland there is only the briefest mention of Dermot Mac Murrough's return. Left unsaid was the fact that he came in the company of only a few followers and without Strongbow. Unnoted, too, was the apprehension with which his arrival was greeted among the likes of Tigernán O'Rourke and the ard-rí Rory O'Connor. In fact, both kings acted quickly to bring Dermot to heel, and Dermot, aware that the bulk of his strength still lay on the far side of the Irish Sea, readily submitted. What he needed now was time, and if he had to buy it

suddenly filled with sails. In league with some 200 knights and another 1,000 men-at-arms, Strongbow had come, to honor his pledge to Dermot, to claim his bride, and to bend to his will the course of Irish history.

But plans, no matter how well laid, do go awry, and by the following spring Dermot was himself unexpectedly dead and, with him, his dream of making his own destiny aligned with that of his country. There would be no high kingship for him, no single kingdom embracing all of Ireland. More ominously, in that same year of 1171, Henry II, envious of Strongbow's conquest and covetous as always of Ireland, would himself arrive in Waterford, to grip more tightly with his right hand what he had grabbed with his left.

masterpieces
of metalwork

For most members of early Irish society, a man's success was measured by the number of cattle he owned. Among the more well-to-do, however, personal ornamentation also signified a person's wealth and status. Brooches, for example, the typically Irish pins worn at the shoulders to fasten a cloak or other clothing, were worn by nearly everyone in the eighth and ninth centuries AD and so served as a ready indicator of the excess wealth an individual might possess. These brooches ranged from the very humblest bronze, a copper alloy, to the most elaborate versions of silver and gold, finely worked and decorated, and set with stones, glass, and enamel.

Ireland's fine metalworking tradition started with the discovery of copper around 2000 BC. Gold was also available at a very early date and was used to fashion treasures such as the showy collars called gorgets and the hair ornaments known as lock rings. The Celtic La Tène culture, which flourished on the Continent from the fifth to the first centuries BC, contributed a style of design to the repertoire of Irish metalworkers that was characterized by bright colors and swirling abstract motifs. Influenced further by the Vikings, Irish artisans incorporated Scandinavian animal art into their designs, ultimately creating a unique and beautiful fusion of styles.

Metalworkers enjoyed an elevated status in Irish society. Some were attached to the courts of chiefs, but others were itinerant practitioners. After Christianization, most metalworkers were monks laboring in monastic workshops. Although the monks were producing Christian liturgical objects, their designs and technique continued to reflect their Celtic origins.

TARA BROOCH
ca. AD 700
Filigree, enamel, amber, golden granules, and glass adorn both sides of this gilded silver pin, the so-called Tara Brooch. Used to fasten a cloak at the shoulder, the pin has a knitted chain that might have connected with a twin brooch or served as a guard. The brooch is shown at actual size, as are all of the objects on the following pages.

"Two tresses of
yellow gold she had,
and each tress was
a weaving of four
twists with a globe
at the end."

124

BRONZE AGE

GOLD DRESS FASTENER
ca. 700 BC

This massive gold dress fastener consists of a bowed handle with buttonlike terminals at each end. To fasten a garment, the terminals were slipped through a double buttonhole made of opposing loops.

GOLD GORGET
ca. 700 BC

Known as a gorget, this collar was fashioned from a single sheet of hammered gold; the decorative disks were stitched to the collar with gold wire. Unique to Ireland, this type of gorget was worn on the chest with the disks resting on the shoulders.

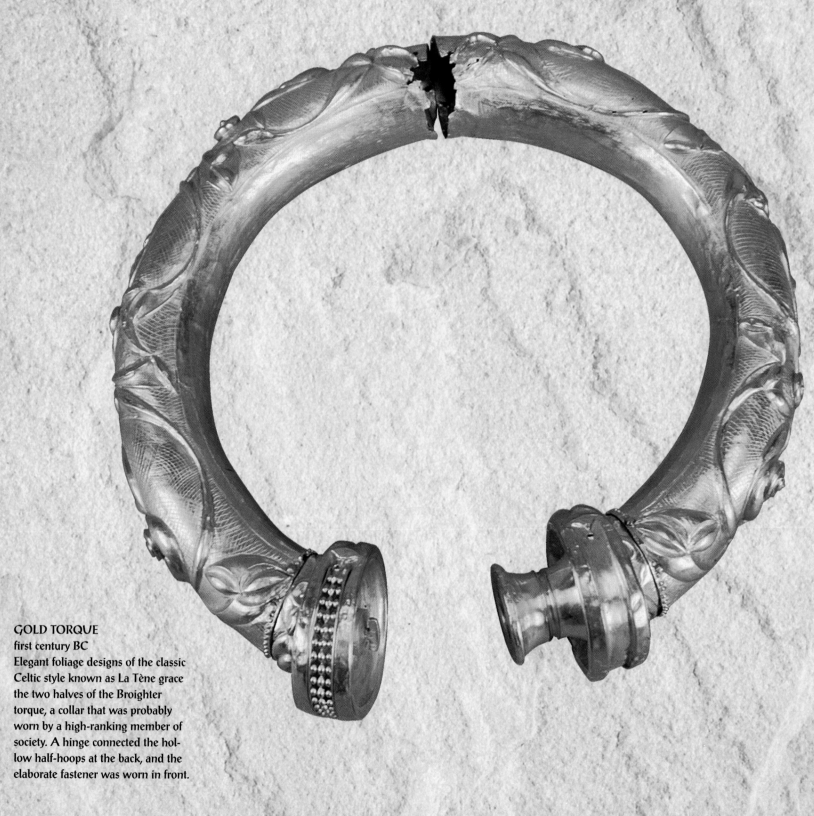

GOLD TORQUE
first century BC
Elegant foliage designs of the classic
Celtic style known as La Tène grace
the two halves of the Broighter
torque, a collar that was probably
worn by a high-ranking member of
society. A hinge connected the hol-
low half-hoops at the back, and the
elaborate fastener was worn in front.

celtic

HANDPINS
AD 500-600
So called because they resemble hands held up with the fingers bent at right angles, handpins were used as decorative cloak fasteners.

BRONZE FASTENER
AD 400-600
A bronze dress fastener, its curved stem designed to slip through slits in a garment, is decorated with triskeles, branches radiating from a center *(detail, right)*. The design was produced by cutting away some metal; the grooves were once filled with red enamel.

"Around their wrists and arms they wear bracelets, and around their necks heavy necklaces of solid gold, and huge rings they wear as well, and even corselets of gold."

ARDAGH CHALICE
ca. AD 700

Richly ornamented with filigree and enameling, the Ardagh communion chalice probably belonged to a wealthy monastery. The engraved names of the apostles circle the vessel. A polished crystal under the stem *(detail, above)* would have been seen by the priest as he raised the cup toward heaven for consecration.

**CAST-BRONZE
DOOR HANDLE**
ca. AD 700
A cast-bronze animal head grasps in its mouth a door handle worn smooth from use. Beautifully decorated and modeled with care, the beast sports amber eyes, finely formed teeth, and spiraling hairs growing out of its snout.

*"Patrick took with him
across the Shannon fifty bells, fifty patens,
fifty chalices, altar-stones, books of the law,
books of the Gospels,
and left them in new places."*

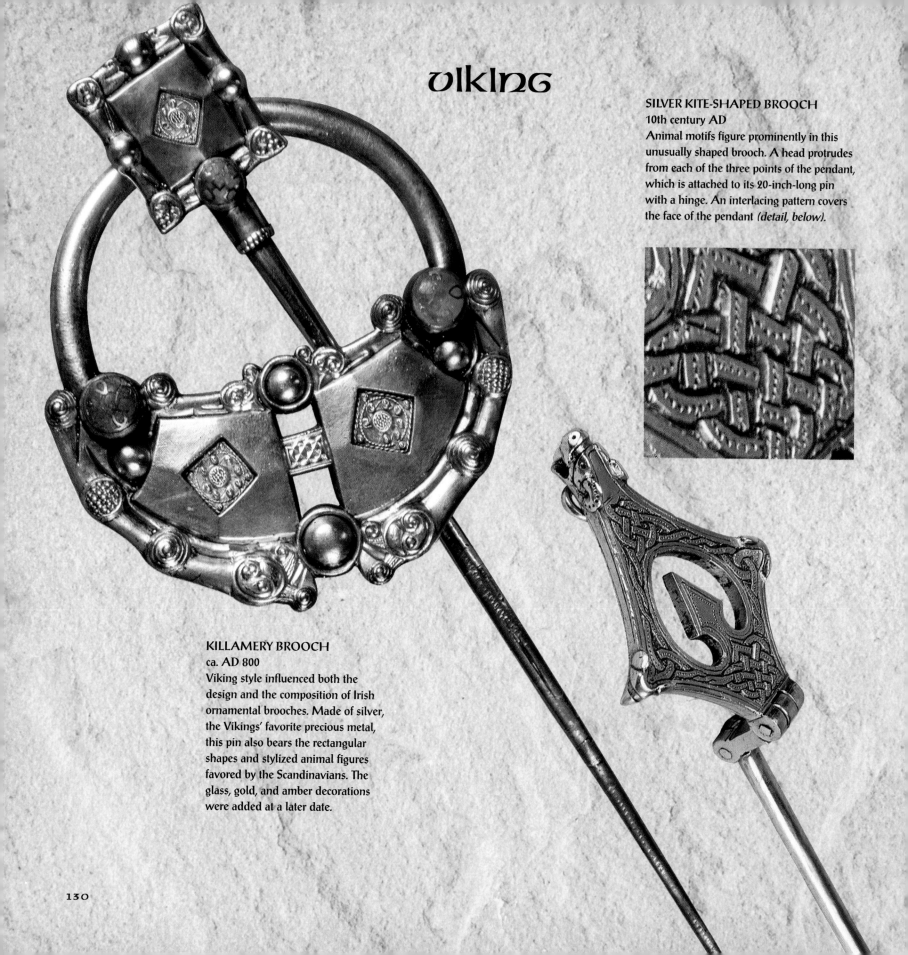

SILVER KITE-SHAPED BROOCH
10th century AD
Animal motifs figure prominently in this unusually shaped brooch. A head protrudes from each of the three points of the pendant, which is attached to its 20-inch-long pin with a hinge. An interlacing pattern covers the face of the pendant *(detail, below)*.

KILLAMERY BROOCH
ca. AD 800
Viking style influenced both the design and the composition of Irish ornamental brooches. Made of silver, the Vikings' favorite precious metal, this pin also bears the rectangular shapes and stylized animal figures favored by the Scandinavians. The glass, gold, and amber decorations were added at a later date.

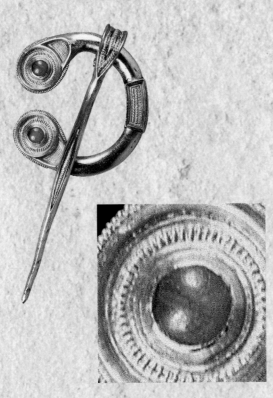

ERVEY BROOCH
ca. AD 800
Made of silver, this brooch has a
disk-shaped terminal at either end
of the ring. In the center of each
is a brown glass stud surrounded
by finely worked cast-gilt rope
molding *(detail, above).*

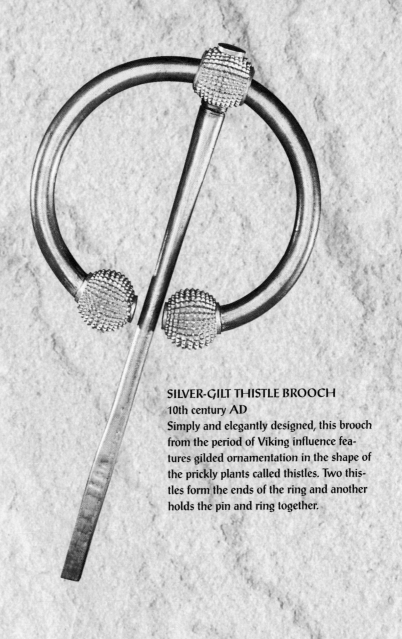

SILVER-GILT THISTLE BROOCH
10th century AD
Simply and elegantly designed, this brooch
from the period of Viking influence features gilded ornamentation in the shape of
the prickly plants called thistles. Two thistles form the ends of the ring and another
holds the pin and ring together.

*"He wore a purple mantle
wrapped around him with a brooch
inlaid with gold over his white breast."*

LISMORE CROSIER
ca. AD 1100
Made for the bishop of Lismore, this cast-bronze crosier was originally covered with panels of gold. Animals, a human head, and glass beads adorn the crook and shaft, and an inscription offers a prayer for both the bishop and the crosier's craftsman.

"The people and clergy
. . . of Ireland have a great
reverence for . . .
staffs belonging to the
saints, and made of
gold and silver, or
bronze, and curved at
their upper ends."

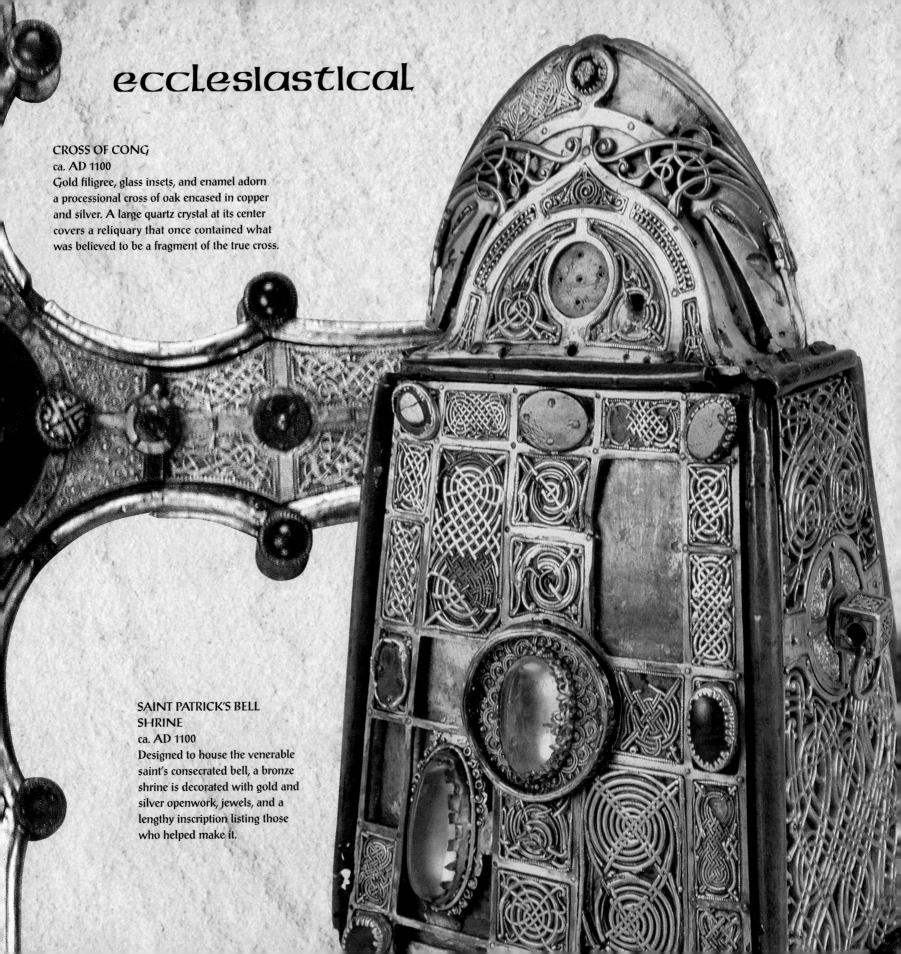

ecclesiastical

CROSS OF CONG
ca. AD 1100
Gold filigree, glass insets, and enamel adorn
a processional cross of oak encased in copper
and silver. A large quartz crystal at its center
covers a reliquary that once contained what
was believed to be a fragment of the true cross.

**SAINT PATRICK'S BELL
SHRINE**
ca. AD 1100
Designed to house the venerable
saint's consecrated bell, a bronze
shrine is decorated with gold and
silver openwork, jewels, and a
lengthy inscription listing those
who helped make it.

Glossary

Abbot: the superior of a monastery.

Ard-rí: in Irish mythology and history, the high king of Ireland.

Beltane: the pagan Irish festival held May 1 celebrating the arrival of summer and the return of livestock to open, high pasture land.

Bóaire: "cattle lord"; a freeman farmer who possessed about eight acres of land.

Body price: compensation paid by a murderer or by his kin group to the family of the victim. An "honor price" that varied according to status was also paid to the victim's family.

Booleying: the act of transferring cattle from winter quarters to communal summer pastures in the mountains.

Cairn: a mound of stones, erected as a marker or memorial.

Carpet pages: in illuminated manuscripts, highly decorative pages prefacing each of the gospels. When a cross was incorporated in the decoration, the page was also called a cross page.

Celtic tonsure: a haircut worn by Irish monks in which the top of the head was shaved forward of a line running from ear to ear with the hair allowed to grow long in the back.

Celts: warrior-farmers, originally of central Europe, who spread through western Europe and into Britain and Ireland during pre-Roman times.

Chalice: a cup or goblet, especially one used for the consecrated wine of the Eucharist.

Chief wife: the first woman that a man married. Under Irish law, he could subsequently marry other women as well, but they would be considered concubines or secondary wives, with only half the status and rights of the chief wife.

Client: one who enters into a clientship relationship with a lord.

Clientship: in Ireland, the system under which a nobleman or lord supplied livestock (and possibly land) to a farmer (his client) in return for stipulated goods and services, including labor and military service.

Cloisonné: a form of ornamental work in which the surface decoration is formed by different colors of enamel separated by thin strips of metal or wire.

Concubine: in Ireland, a secondary wife, with lower social status and fewer rights than the primary wife.

Coracle: a small, round-bottomed boat covered with animal hide stretched over a wicker or wooden frame.

Cosmology: the theory used by a culture to explain their antecedents, ancient history, world, and supreme beings, and the manner in which these act and interact.

Coulter: on a plow, an iron blade or knife, mounted vertically in front of the iron plowshare, that makes vertical cuts in the sod and soil, enabling the plowshare to create a deeper furrow in the soil.

Crannog: a natural or artificial fortified island refuge in a lake or bog.

Crosier: a staff with a cross or crook on the top, often highly decorated, carried by or before an abbot, bishop, or archbishop as a symbol of his office.

Divination: the art or act of foretelling the future by observing human and animal behavior and natural phenomena.

Dolmens: megalithic structures from the Neolithic Age consisting of two or more upright stones covered with a capstone, typically forming a single chamber; originally covered with a mound of earth and probably used as tombs.

Druids: members of the pagan Irish learned class, a combination of priest, prophet, sorcerer, healer, judge, educator, and astrologer, with divination being one of their most important functions; wielded immense influence and power over both religious and political affairs.

Druid's fence: a means by which druids, according to some chroniclers, could protect the warriors of their army from those of the opposing army by erecting a barrier between them.

Eire: the name by which modern Ireland is known; evolved from the name of the Irish goddess Ériu.

Emain Macha: in Irish mythology, the royal stronghold of the war goddess Macha. Probably situated at the modern Navan Fort near Armagh, and occupied since at least 700 BC, Emain Macha was said to be the seat of the royal court of the mythological kings of Ulster and the stronghold of the warrior-hero Connor Mac Nessa. One of the most sacred sites in Celtic Ireland.

Fealty: an oath of fidelity and assistance owed by a vassal to his lord and the protection owed by the lord to his vassal.

Fifths: the five historical provinces of Ireland: Ulster, Munster, Leinster, Connacht, and Meath.

Filidh: the learned poets of early Ireland, members of an intellectual elite who performed both secular and religious roles and who acted as the repository and conveyers of the oral tradition of Irish mythology, history, and genealogy.

Filigree: delicate and intricate ornamentation, originally made of beads or grains of gold or silver, later made of fine, twisted wire.

Fine: a kinship group, larger than the immediate family of parents and siblings, which represented four generations of male kinsmen, typically including all male descendants of a common great-grandfather; the basic law-enforcement and land-holding unit in the Irish economy.

Fír flathemon: literally, "the king's truth or justice," which was believed to ward off all manner of evils during the reign of a good king.

Flax: a slender erect annual plant cultivated for its fiber, which is used to make linen.

Flesh fork: a fork used in the cooking and eating of meat.

Fosterage: the practice, especially among wealthier families and the nobility, of sending young sons and daughters to the home of another for child rearing and training.

Freeman: a person not in slavery or serfdom, possessing full legal rights within the tribe.

Fulling: increasing the weight, density, and softness of wool by moistening, heating, and pressing.

Gaul: the name for the territory now known as France; the last Celtic stronghold in continental Europe, which fell in 52 BC to Julius Caesar.

Gaels: another name for the Irish.

Gorget: a collar worn with upper body armor to protect the throat; in Ireland, an ornamental metal collar that rested on the shoulders.

Hack silver: silver fragments hacked from coins, necklaces, and armbands and used as a medium of exchange according to the fragments' weight and value.

Handpins: elongated stick pins with heads resembling hands, used as decorative cloak fasteners.

Heroic age: in Irish mythology, the period said to have begun about the time of the birth of Christ and continuing for several centuries during which a warrior society flourished in Ireland, the exploits of which are chronicled in the Ulster Cycle.

High crosses: freestanding, usually highly carved and decorated stone crosses, erected as early as the sixth century and for several centuries thereafter.

Honor price: the payment made by a murderer or his kin group to the family of the victim, based on the status of the victim and his or her family, the closeness of their relationship, and the sex of the victim. A body price was also paid to the victim's family.

Imbas forosna: literally, "the knowledge that enlightens." In Irish lore, a ritual performed to foretell the future.

Imbolc: one of the major pagan Irish festivals, held annually on February 1, to herald the advent of spring.

Keltoi: ancient Greek word for the Celtic peoples of Europe.

Kingship: the position, power, or province of a king; in Ireland, a loosely hierarchical structure with several different levels of kings: the king of the túath (who ruled only his own túath), the *ruiri* (who was overlord of his own túath and several others as well), and the *rí ruirech* (the king of a province). Over all of these kings was the *ard-rí,* or high king.

La Tène: the Celtic Iron Age civilization that flourished in continental Europe from the fifth to the first centuries BC and that continued in Ireland into the Christian era; the classic Celtic style.

Legion: the major unit of the Roman army, consisting originally of 3,000 (later 6,000) infantry troops and between 100 and 300 cavalry troops.

Lia Fáil: the Stone of Destiny. In Irish mythology, a stone brought to Tara as one of four magical talismans of the Túatha Dé Danaan. It shrieked when touched by the rightful high king of Ireland.

Liegeman: a vassal, loyal supporter, or subject.

Linen: thread made from fibers from the flax plant; cloth woven from this thread.

Loch: a lake or arm of the sea similar to a fjord.

Lock rings: hair ornaments with bosses on the inside of a center tube that secured the hair.

Longship: a type of Viking ship with a single sail and a continuous row of oars on each side, used by the Vikings for warfare, raiding parties, and exploring.

Lord: a man of high rank in medieval society, especially a king, nobleman, or landowner with extensive property; in early Ireland, one who granted livestock (and possibly land) to a farmer (client) in return for stipulated goods and services, including labor and military service.

Lughnasadh: one of the major Celtic festivals of Ireland, celebrated on August 1 and associated both with the god Lugh and with the beginning of the harvest.

Mac: an Irish prefix meaning "son of," added to the personal name of the father (or occasionally the mother), originally changing with each generation but eventually becoming a hereditary family surname.

Mead: an alcoholic beverage made of fermented honey and water.

Megaliths: "great stones"; huge stones or boulders used in constructing monuments.

Mercenaries: professional soldiers hired for service in a foreign army or an army of another tribe or province.

Mether: a communal drinking vessel, passed among friends, from which ale was drunk.

Monastery: a community of persons bound by vows to a religious life and often living in partial or complete seclusion; the dwelling place of such a community.

Monk: a man who belongs to a religious order.

Navel of Ireland: Uisneach, also called the Stone of Divisions; the site was thought to mark the point where Irish provinces met.

Newgrange: a megalithic passage grave from the Neolithic Age, part of a prehistoric complex of tombs near the River Boyne built around 3100 BC; depicted in Irish mythology as an entrance to the otherworld and as the dwelling place of the god Óengus.

Nun: a woman who enters a convent and takes holy orders. In Ireland, a nun sometimes had legal rights unavailable to other women, stemming both from her status as a nun and, if her family's tinól was generous, as a woman of wealth.

O: an Irish prefix meaning "male descendant" and eventually "grandson of"; added to the personal name of the grandfather. Originally changing with each generation, it later became a hereditary family surname.

Ócaire: a small farmer who owned, according to law tracts, four acres, seven cows, one bull, seven pigs, seven sheep, and a horse.

Oénach: assembly of people from one or more túaths at which public business was conducted and trade, festivities, and games took place.

Ogham: the 20-character alphabet used in Ireland from the fifth to the seventh century, consisting of inscribed grooves or strokes set at different angles to a vertical line; said to have been inspired by Ogma, god of eloquence.

Otherworld: often identified with the underground kingdom of the Túatha Dé Danaan after their defeat by the Celts, characterized as a land of enchantment.

Palisade: a fence of pointed wooden stakes (pales) forming a defensive barrier, sometimes built atop an earthern embankment to afford it extra protection from intruders.

Pallet: a narrow, hard bed, straw mat, or mattress.

Passage graves: also known as passage tombs, or sídh. Neolithic burial tombs consisting of long, narrow passages leading to one or more burial chambers, created long before the coming of the Celts, but assimilated by them into their mythology as sídh or otherworld dwellings.

Pilgrimage: a journey to a holy place or shrine, undertaken as a demonstration of devotion or as an act of penance.

Portal tombs: a burial chamber framed by upright boulders and a massive capstone; also known as dolmens.

Province: five historical divisions of Ireland: Ulster, Munster, Leinster, Connacht, and Meath.

Quill: a writing instrument made from a feather shaft.

Rath: another name for a ring-fort.

Reliquary: a small bag, casket, or other container in which sacred relics, such as the clothing or bones of a dead saint, were kept or displayed.

Ring-fort: a rath; a circular fortified area consisting of an earthen embankment and ditch that provided some protection against wild animals and thieves and within which one or more family homes were located.

Rí ruirech: "king of great nobles"; probably a term for a provincial king.

Ruiri: a "great king"; king of his own túath as well as overlord of three or four other túatha.

Samhain: one of the four major pagan Irish festivals; celebrated November 1, it marked the return of herds from summer pasture, the end of summer, the onset of winter, and the beginning of a new year.

Scabbard: a sheath for a sword.

Scribe (Scriba): in a monastery, a monk who copied manuscripts.

Scripture cross: a type of Irish high cross that is carved on all sides with scenes from the Old and New Testaments.

Scythe: a tool with a long, curved single-edged blade and a long bent handle used in harvesting grain.

Sét: a unit of measure and exchange, with one sét equal to half a milk cow.

Sheela-na-gigs: grotesque stone carvings of female figures, usually found on churches.

Sickle: a tool with a semicircular blade attached to a short handle, used in harvesting grain.

Sídh: the Irish word for "fairy mound"; in Irish mythology, said to be the homes of the Túatha Dé Danaan and gateways to the otherworld but in actuality, ancient burial mounds of the Neolithic and Bronze Ages.

Slave: a worker bound in servitude as the property of another, with no legal rights or protection.

Slave belt: a special belt worn by Irish slaves as a token of their slavery.

Smith: one who forges iron into tools and weapons; in Irish society, regarded as possessing supernatural powers.

Solstice: either of two times of the year when the sun is farthest from the celestial equator.

Sons of a living father: in Ireland, the legal category by which sons were classified until after the death of their father, when they would receive their inheritance of land and cease being dependents subject to the authority of their father.

Spit: a slender, pointed iron rod for holding meat over a fire.

Standing stones: one of several types of Neolithic monuments; stones of this sort were used to mark boundaries and burial places, occurring singly or in alignment with one another.

Stone circles: a cluster of Neolithic standing stones with the monumental stones arranged in a circle; considered to be sacred sites by the Irish.

Stone of Divisions: another name for the Navel of Ireland.

Stone rows: standing megalithic stones arranged in a row.

Summer food: butter and cheese, available only during the summer after the livestock gave birth and the cows began producing milk.

Táin: a cattle raid.

Tara: a 500-foot-high grassy hill in the Boyne Valley in the province of Meath, described in early literature as containing a complex of buildings on or around the hill, considered a sacred site in Irish mythology and history.

Thatch: a type of covering for a roof made of straw, rushes, reeds, or leaves.

Tigerna: literally, "lord." Originally, a minor king, leader of a túath; by the eighth century, diminished in power and influence to that of a local lord.

Timpán: a stringed musical instrument frequently referred to in Irish tales.

Tinól: in a union of joint property, the marriage property contributed equally by both partners or their families to the new household; it usually included tools and implements for both female and male tasks.

Torque: an ornamental neck ring, possibly imbued with magical and religious significance, worn by people of high status and frequently depicted around the necks of Celtic gods and goddesses.

Trews: tight trousers reaching below the knee, worn by Irish soldiers.

Triskele: a decorative design consisting of three gracefully curved lines or branches radiating from a common center, frequently found on disks or flat surfaces of jewelry.

Túath: (plural: túatha) the most basic unit of governance in early Ireland, in essence an extended family group or tribe, each with its own king, who occupied the lowest rung on the ladder of Irish kingship.

Tuísech: literally, "leader"; a minor king, leader of a túath.

Tunic: a loose-fitting, knee-length linen garment cinched at the waist with a leather belt, worn in early medieval Ireland by both women and men.

Uisneach: the "Navel of Ireland"; the point where the Irish provinces of Ulster, Munster, Leinster, and Connacht were said to meet.

Ulster Cycle: a group of legends and stories about the heroic age of the people of Ulster, set around the time of Christ. Many of these tales may have had their origins in oral tradition, but attained written form between the eighth and 12th centuries.

Undutiful son: a son who, contrary to his responsibility under Irish law, did not take care of his parents in their declining years.

Union of joint property: one of the nine different forms of sexual union recognized by Irish law and the most prestigious and advantageous to the bride, based upon the contribution by both partners of an equal amount of marriage property, thus making her, under the law, "a woman of equal lordship."

Vassal: a feudal tenant, subject, dependent, subordinate, or sometimes, a slave of a lord.

Vellum: a thin, supple material made of calfskin used for the pages and bindings of books.

Vikings: any of the seafaring people from Denmark, Sweden, and Norway, who, beginning in 795, periodically raided Irish monasteries and who eventually settled in Ireland.

Wattle: a construction method in which poles are woven with twigs, reeds, or branches; used for walls and fences.

Wattle and daub: a construction method in which wattle is covered with a mixture of clay or mud.

Western Sea: another name for the Atlantic Ocean.

Whey: the watery part of milk that separates from the curds during the cheesemaking process, used as a beverage.

Winter food: food eaten during the winter, when milk, butter, fruits, and vegetables were not available; specifically, salted or cured beef, salt pork, sausage, and smoked bacon.

Woman of equal lordship: in Irish law, the status accorded a woman by a union of joint property, in essence, recognizing her as an equal partner, economically and legally, with her husband in the management of their property and business affairs.

pronunciation guide

Achtán (AK-tawn)
Adomnán (ADH-ov-non)
Ailill (AL-ill)
Amlaíb Cuaráin (AHV-liv KOOAR-oihn)
ard-rí (ARD-ree)
Armagh (AR-mah)
Athlone (ATH-lohn)
bóaire (BOAH-ruh)
Boru (BOH-roo)
Brega (BRAY-yuh)
Brethán (BREH-thahn)
Brodir (BROH-dir)
cárthach (KAHR-thuch)
Cathach (KAH-thuch)
Clíodna (KLEE-udh-nuh)
Coemgen (KOHV-yen)
Connacht (KON-not)
Connor Mac Nessa (KON-air MAK NES-sah)
Cormac Mac Airt (KOR-muhk MAK AIHRT)
Croagh (KROH)
Cruachan Aigle (KROO-ak-huhn EYE-luh)
Cu Chulainn (KOO HOOL-in)
Dál Cais (DAWL GASH)
Derbforgaill (DARE-vor-gil)
Derryaghy (DAYREE-ah-gee)
Diarmaid (DEER-muhd)
Donaghadee (DON-ahg-ah-DEE)
Donncadh (DONN-ah-cah)
Eóganacht (OH-uh-nakt)
Ériu (AY-ryoo)
eigerna (AYR-nuh)
Fearghaíl (FARE-yuhl)
Fíachnae Cassán (FEE-ak-nah CAS-sahn)
fír flathemon (FIR FLAHTH-uh-vwehn)

filidh (FIL-idh)
fine (FIN-uh)
Fomhoire (FO-wuh-re)
Glendalough (GLEN-duh-lawk)
Gormlaith (GORM-lahth)
Gráinne (GRAN-nya)
Gríanán of Ailech (GREE-A-nawn of AH-lehk)
Killyleagh (KIL-lee-LAY)
Knocknagoney (NOK-nah-GOHN-ee)
Leinster (LEN-stuhr)
Lia Fáil (LEE-ah FOYL)
Lóeg (LOYGH)
Loégaire (LOY-ya-ruh)
Lough Neagh (LAWK NAY)
Lucet Máel (LOO-ket MAYL)
Lugaid (LOO-gudh)
Lughnasadh (LOO-nuh-sa)
Máel Sechnaill (MAYL SHEK-nil)
Mac an Bháird (MAK un WAHRD)
Mac Cárthaigh (MAK KAHR-thee)
Mac Conchobair (MAK KAHNK-oh-vuhr)
Mac Giolla Bhríghde (MAK GIL-lah VREEG-dhuh)
Mac Giolla Phádraiga (MAK GIL-lah FAW-dri-guh)
Mac Lochlainn (MAK LAWK-lahn)
Macha (MAH-chuh)
Mag Luinge (MAG LUIN-geh)
Mag Uidhir (MAG EE-thir)
Magh n-Elda (MAG nuh-EL-duh)
Míall (MEE-yahl)
Mochuda (MO-KOO-dah)
Muirchertach Mac Loughlin (MWIR-cher-dahk MAK LAWK-lin)

Mumhan (MOH-uhn)
Murchad (MUR-kahdh)
Núadha (NOO-uh-dhuh)
Ó Bríain (OH BREE-uhn)
Ó Cennétig (OH KEN-nay-dee)
Ó Cléirigh (OH KLAY-ree)
Ó Coinn (OH KOIN)
Ó Dálaigh (OH DAWL-ee)
Ó Floinn (OH FLINN)
Ó Tuathail (OH TOO-uth-uhl)
ócaire (OH-guh-ruh)
Óchter Achid (OHK-tehr AHK-idh)
Oénach (OH-a-nahk)
Ó hAonghasa (OH-HANG-gus-suh)
Olc Aiche (OHLK EE-che)
rí ruirech (REE RUR-ech)
ruiri (RUR-ee)
Samhain (SAWV-win)
scriba (SKREE-buh)
sét (SHADE)
sídh (SHEE)
Sitriuc (SIT-ryuhk)
Strigiul (STRIG-yul)
Táin Bó Cuailnge (TOYN BOH COO-ling-ah)
Taoiseach (TEE-shahk)
Temair na Ríg (TEU-ur nah REE)
Tigernán O'Rourke (TEE-yur-nahn OH-ROHRK)
tinól (TI-nohl)
Tiree (TIE-ree)
Túatha Dé Danaan (TOO-uh-thuh day DAH-nuhn)
tuísech (TEE-shahk)
Turlough (TUR-low)
Uí Néill (EE NYAY-ull)

acknowledgments

The editors wish to thank the following individuals and institutions for their valuable assistance in the preparation of this volume:

Valerie Dowling, National Museum of Ireland, Dublin; Christopher Dunin-Borkowski, London; Sharon Fogarty, National Museum of Ireland, Dublin; Rhona Gyles, National Museum of Ireland, Dublin; Fritz-Rudolf Herrmann, Landesamt für Denkmalpflege Hessen, Wiesbaden, Germany; John Kennedy, Blackrock, Co. Dublin, Ireland; Heidrun Klein, Bildarchiv Preussischer Kulturbesitz, Berlin; Sean and Dr. Janina Lyons, Blanchardstown, Co. Dublin, Ireland; Pat McLean, Ulster Museum, Belfast, Northern Ireland; Susan O'Regan, National Museum of Ireland, Dublin; Michelle O'Riordan, School of Celtic Studies, Dublin Institute for Advanced Studies, Dublin, Ireland; Erika Partsch; Landesamt für Denkmalpflege Hessen, Wiesbaden, Germany.

BIBLIOGRAPHY

BOOKS

Arnold, Bruce. *Irish Art: A Concise History.* London: Thames and Hudson, 1977.

Backhouse, Janet. *The Lindisfarne Gospels.* Oxford: Phaidon, 1981.

Batey, Colleen, et al. *Cultural Atlas of the Viking World.* Ed. by James Graham-Campbell. New York: Facts On File, 1994.

Bethu Brigte. Ed. by Donncha Ó hAodha. Dublin: Dublin Institute for Advanced Studies, 1978.

Bieler, Ludwig, trans. and ed. *The Patrician Texts in the Book of Armagh.* Dublin: Dublin Institute for Advanced Studies, 1979.

Bruun, Johan Adolf. *The Book of Kells.* London: Studio Editions, 1986.

Cairney, C. Thomas. *Clans and Families of Ireland and Scotland: An Ethnography of the Gael, A.D. 500-1750.* Jefferson, N.C.: McFarland & Co., 1989.

The Celts. Milan: Bompiani, 1991.

Constable, Nick. *Ancient Ireland.* Edison, N.J.: Chartwell Books, 1996.

Cunliffe, Barry. *The Celtic World.* New York: St. Martin's Press, 1990.

Dames, Michael. *Mythic Ireland.* London: Thames and Hudson, 1992.

Duane, O. B. *Celtic Art.* New York: Barnes & Noble, 1996.

Dunlevy, Mairead. *Dress in Ireland.* New York: Holmes & Meier, 1989.

Edwards, Nancy. *The Archaeology of Early Medieval Ireland.* Philadelphia: University of Pennsylvania Press, 1990.

Ellis, Peter Berresford. *The Druids.* Grand Rapids: William B. Eerdmans, 1994.

Eluère, Christiane. *The Celts: Conquerors of Ancient Europe.* New York: Harry N. Abrams, 1993.

Farmer, David Hugh. *The Oxford Dictionary of Saints.* Oxford: Oxford University Press, 1992.

Figures from the Past: Studies on Figurative Art in Christian Ireland. Ed. by Etienne Rynne. Dublin: Glendale Press, 1987.

Gantz, Jeffrey, trans. *Early Irish Myths and Sagas.* New York: Penguin Books, 1981.

Gaur, Albertine. *A History of Writing.* London: British Library, 1984.

Giraldus Cambrensis (Gerald of Wales):
The History and Topography of Ireland. Trans. by John J. O'Meara. New York: Penguin Books, 1982.
The History and Topography of Ireland. Trans. by John J. O'Meara. Mountrath, Portlaoise, Ireland: Dolmen Press, 1982 (rev. ed.).

Green, Miranda Aldhouse:
Celtic Art: Reading the Messages. London: Calmann & King, 1996.
Celtic Goddesses: Warriors, Virgins and Mothers. London: British Museum Press, 1995.

Grenham, John. *Clans and Families of Ireland: The Heritage and Heraldry of Irish Clans and Families.* Dublin: Gill and Macmillan, 1993.

Harbison, Peter:
Pilgrimage in Ireland. Syracuse, N.Y.: Syracuse University Press, 1991.
Pre-Christian Ireland: From the First Settlers to the Early Celts. London: Thames and Hudson, 1988.

Higgins, Godfrey. *The Celtic Druids.* Los Angeles: Philosophical Research Society, 1977 (reprint of 1829 edition).

Hughes, Kathleen. *The Church in Early Irish Society.* London: Methuen, 1966.

The Irish World: The History and Cultural Achievements of the Irish People. Ed. by Brian De Breffny. London: Thames and Hudson, 1997.

James, Simon. *The World of the Celts.* London: Thames and Hudson, 1993.

Kelly, Eamonn P.:
Early Celtic Art in Ireland. Dublin: National Museum of Ireland, 1993.
Sheela-na-Gigs: Origins and Functions. Dublin: Country House, 1996.

Kelly, Sean, and Rosemary Rogers. *Saints Preserve Us!: Everything You Need to Know about Every Saint You'll Ever Need.* New York: Random House, 1993.

Kissane, Noel, ed. *Treasures from the National Library of Ireland.* London: Alpine Fine Arts Collection, 1995.

Kruta, Venceslas. *The Celts of the West.* Trans. by Alan Sheridan. London: Orbis, 1985.

Laing, Lloyd, and Jennifer Laing. *Art of the Celts.* London: Thames and Hudson, 1992.

Mac Cana, Proinsias. *Celtic Mythology.* London: Hamlyn Publishing, 1970.

Mallory, J. P., ed. *Aspects of the Táin.* Belfast: December Publications, 1992.

Matthew, Donald. *Atlas of Medieval Europe.* New York: Facts On File, 1983.

Meehan, Bernard. *The Book of Kells: An Illustrated Introduction to the Manuscript in Trinity College Dublin.* London: Thames and Hudson, 1994.

The Mystic Dawn: Celtic Europe (Myth and the Imagination of Mankind series). Amsterdam: Time-Life Books BV, 1996.

National Geographic Atlas of the World. Washington, D.C.: National Geographic Society, 1970.

Neill, Kenneth. *The Irish People: An Illustrated History.* New York: Mayflower Books, 1979.

O'Brien, Jacqueline, and Peter Harbison. *Ancient Ireland: From Prehistory to the Middle Ages.* New York: Oxford University Press, 1996.

Ó Catháin, Séamas. *The Festival of Brigit: Celtic Goddess and Holy Woman.* London: Longman, 1995.

Ó Cróinín, Dáibhí. *Early Medieval Ireland: 400-1200.* Dublin: DBA Publications, 1995.

Ó Floinn, Raghnall. *Irish Shrines & Reliquaries of the Middle Ages.* Dublin: National Museum of Ireland, 1994.

O'Kelly, Michael J. *Newgrange: Archaeology, Art and Legend.* London: Thames and Hudson, 1982.

The Oxford Illustrated History of Ireland. Ed. by R. F. Foster. Oxford: Oxford University Press, 1989.

Pennick, Nigel. *Celtic Sacred Landscapes.* New York: Thames and Hudson, 1996.

Raftery, Barry. *Pagan Celtic Ireland.* London: Thames and Hudson, 1994.

Roberts, Timothy R. *The Celts in Myth and Legend.* New York: Friedman/Fairfax, MetroBooks, 1995.

Ryan, Michael. *Metal Craftsmanship in Early Ireland.* Dublin: Country House, 1993.

Ryan, Michael, ed.:
The Illustrated Archaeology of Ireland. Dublin: Country House, 1991.
Irish Archaeology Illustrated. Dublin: Country House, 1994.

Scherman, Katharine. *The Flowering of Ireland: Saints, Scholars, and Kings.* New York: Barnes & Noble, 1981.

Sharkey, John. *Celtic Mysteries: The Ancient Religion.* London: Thames and Hudson, 1975.

The Times Atlas of the World. New York: Times Books, 1980.

The Times Atlas of World History. Ed. by Geoffrey Barraclough. Maplewood, N.J.: Hammond, 1993.

Treasures of Early Irish Art: 1500 B.C. to 1500 A.D. New York: Metropolitan Museum of Art, 1977.

Treasures of Ireland: Irish Art 3000 B.C. to 1500 A.D. Dublin: Royal Irish Academy, 1983.

Waddell, Helen. *The Wandering Scholars.* Garden City, N.Y.: Doubleday Anchor Books, 1955.

'The Work of Angels': Masterpieces of Celtic Metalwork, 6th-9th Centuries A.D. Ed. by Susan Youngs. London: British Museum Publications, 1989.

PERIODICALS

"The Viking Issue." *Archæology Ireland,* Autumn 1995.

Index

Numerals in italics indicate an illustration of the subject mentioned.